Meditations on the Vocation of Motherhood

"*Meditations on the Vocation of Motherhood* by Marie K. MacPherson packs both convicting and comforting reflections into conversational devotions for all mothers, whether new or seasoned. Each meditation begins with a carefully chosen Scripture passage and concludes with a meaningfully poetic hymn stanza. Old and New Testament selections are suggested for further study.

"Honest, thoughtful, and personal, *Meditations on the Vocation of Motherhood* faithfully commends the reader to our only Lord and Savior Jesus Christ. Raised by Christian parents, educated in Lutheran schools K-college, and now writing as a mother of five, Marie admits that perhaps more than anything, her 'own inadequacies' have equipped her to share the comfort she has received from reading God's Word. She offers due gratitude to 'the Father of all mercies and God of all comfort, who comforts us in all our tribulation, that we may be able to comfort...' (2 Corinthians 1:3–4). If you sometimes wish you had a wise woman of faith living next door to you, these meditations will bring the much-needed companionship, sincerity, and wisdom directly into your own calling of motherhood."

Cheryl Swope, M.Ed., author of *Simply Classical: A Beautiful Education for Any Child* (Memoria Press, 2013), creator of the Simply Classical Curriculum (Memoria Press) for special needs, *co-author of Eternal Treasures: Teaching Your Child at Home* (LCMS, 2015), and wife of nearly thirty years, is mother to Michael and Michelle, adult twins with special needs.

"It's common knowledge that 'they grow up fast.' but less commonly acknowledged that the hours can be slow. Marie MacPherson's thoughtful devotions are the perfect habit to accompany the cup of coffee, quick stroll, chat with a friend, and other small oases that help a day along. Her domestic gaze reminds the reader that every person who comes to the Lord's Word comes as His workmanship, including those who come holding the little hands of others."

Rebekah Curtis, wife, mom, occasional writer, and co-author
of *LadyLike: Living Biblically* (CPH, 2015)

"In a world that scorns the traditional family and often mocks the vocation of motherhood, Marie MacPherson has brought forth jewels of wisdom from the Old Testament, and demonstrated how these passages bear specific wisdom, grace, encouragement, and admonition for mothers of all ages. I certainly would not have thought to read some of these passages in the light of my own vocation as a mother, but Mrs. MacPherson has shown me how. For the Lutheran and non-Lutheran mother, mother-to-be, grandmother, or even childless woman who nurtures others, these well written and accessible devotionals are a must-read."

Nicole M. King, Managing Editor of *The Natural Family:
An International Journal of Research and Policy*

"In her introduction, Marie MacPherson states, 'You don't need to read these meditations. Really! There's nothing here that you can't find in a devotion book written for any and all Christians.' She's right. You don't need to add one more thing to your reading list nor feel any guilt about not having time to read this devotion book or any others, for that matter. But she's also wrong. You do need to read these. Beautifully written for mothers, Marie writes succinct devotions based on Biblical texts that pinpoint so many of a woman's fears and joys. Pointing to Christ, each devotion will give you thoughts to chew on throughout your day and throughout your life as wife and mother. You don't need to read this book of meditations, but I encourage you to buy it and do so anyway."

Glenda Mumme, mother of five, grandmother of one,
board member of *Wittenberg Academy*

"Lutheran mamas, here is a truly Christ-centered devotional for your everyday life. Bible history, relatable application, and hymn verse are neatly packaged with a comforting, cross-shaped bow holding them all together."

Karyn Lukasek, wife, mother of four, and children's book author/illustrator

"Life is busy. By definition, motherhood is busy, 24/7, yet in a brief moment Marie's book can 'save the day' or at least put it into spiritual perspective. In a minute before rolling out of bed, or while nursing a baby, in the waiting room, while stirring a pot of soup, or just before turning off the bedside lamp, a moment can be snatched to receive the blessing of a Word from God and the consolation of a Sister in Christ. Peace, reassurance and encouragement to carry on are all wrapped up in each little nugget."

Mrs. Rick (LaRena) Stuckwisch, Emmaus Lutheran, South Bend, Ind., mother of ten, grandmother of 7 grandchildren (so far)

"*Meditations on the Vocation of Motherhood* is remarkable for its clear and incisive walk through the Old Testament. MacPherson directs us to the greatest women's spiritual self-help of all time— God's enduring and timeless wisdom, the Bible. She invites us to consider its meaning through the lens of our own unique vocation —motherhood. I appreciate the embedding of hymn excerpts with each meditation. She keeps the meditation brief, but points to further scriptural references for deeper study—when we moms get the discretionary time to dig deeper. This book masterfully directs us to the source of all encouragement, discernment, and support— God's Word."

Julie Quist, wife, mother, grandmother of 47 (so far), and board member of *Child Protection League*

"By pointing the reader to God's Word and the gospel message of salvation, these short and to the point devotions continually lift up the persevering (and sometimes exhausted) mother with assurances of God's almighty love, grace, forgiveness, and eternal presence. What a tool of encouragement these devotions are for the tender mother who gives her all and faces her failings daily!"

Tricia Zahner, mother of six sweet souls, who is
deeply thankful for God's daily forgiveness

"The author is living the joys and challenges of motherhood, wrapped in God's grace through it all. These devotions are a testament to that! The Scripture and brief devotions are ideal for the on-the-go mom; the hymn verses tie it all together. And for those times when you desire a deeper study, continue with the suggested additional readings. So relatable with clear Law and Gospel messages. Just what this mom and wife needs!"

Paula Sulzle, pastor's wife, mom to 6, author, teacher,
volunteer, and small business owner

Meditations on the Vocation of Motherood

Volume 1: Old Testament

Marie K. MacPherson

Editor of *Mothering Many:*
Sanity-Saving Strategies from Moms of Four or More

Into Your Hands LLC

MANKATO, MINN.

2018

Into Your Hands LLC
Mankato, Minnesota
www.intoyourhandsllc.com

Meditations on the Vocation of Motherhood; Volume 1: Old Testament, by Marie K. MacPherson.

ISBN-10: 0-9857543-6-2

ISBN-13: 978-0-9857543-6-5

Library of Congress Subject Headings
Mothers—Prayer books and devotions
Vocation—Lutheran Church
Christian life

Table of Contents

Foreword

Mary J. Moerbe

Mothers are not a homogeneous group, although sometimes they are treated that way. Strangers offer the same advice to every mother they see. Otherwise friendly people shoot judging looks in stores and restaurants, because children have apparently fallen outside societal norms.

Every one of us is different, as are our children. It isn't even surprising, yet so often even mothers are quick to alarm their comrades-in-calling in battles over parenting philosophies and wide-ranging opinions.

I've got good news for you. This set of devotions is content to let you know your own needs and concerns. You won't get yet another dose of unwanted advice or expectations, except that you, too, are a human, Christian, imperfect mother who will benefit from the Gospel and God's Word.

I have a confession to make. I've written for mothers on a number of occasions, even before I had much parenting experience. What I did have was conviction that our good and gracious God sent His Word to earth. That Word offers much needed perspective, wisdom, encouragement, and, yes, correction for all of us, mothers included. This book demonstrates exactly that: God's care is for all His people, and His Word is for mothers in their vocational struggles, too!

The Triune God calls creation into being. He calls us to faith, baptism, and His table. He calls us to trust Himself above all things as the source of every good. And, He calls us to love our neighbors, serving even the smallest whom God has given us, letting us share in His own work of tending and shaping.

There are beautiful simplicities and gifts inherent to motherhood, both in the blessing of receiving a child and in tailoring love to that specific child. And, there are promises which our Lord continues to make and keep.

Mothers are called to raise their children, as simple and as complicated as that is! Mothers are called to be honored and obeyed by their children. Mothers are called to be, and to raise up, workers in God's Kingdom.

While the media meditates on problems with procreation, mommy wars, and battling parenting philosophies, nothing in the world can belittle the tremendous love our God has shown us. He sent His Son to be a child. He makes us His beloved children! He has granted us the tremendous blessing of children! And, He allows us to join Him as He raises up the next generation. Truly, He knows each hair on our family's heads, including those pulled out!

There is so much wisdom, consolation, perspective, encouragement, and commiseration in the Bible and the Liturgy, and that is precisely how this gem of a book fits into the context of you and your vocation as a mother. The text brings you into the family fabric of the Word of God. In roughly chronological order, it brings you through Bible passages offering perspective, speaking truth, and—the most comforting and encouraging aspect of all—giving you sweet Gospel reminders of all Christ has done, and continues to do, for you and your child. Hope, sustenance, and wisdom from Wisdom Himself!

Marie has prepared a book you can read and reread during any stage of parenting. Straight forward language pairs with wise Biblical phrases for simple, enjoyable text. As one sister-in-Christ to another, the author simply offers a little fellowship time around the Word. Those who appreciate the Catechism and Liturgy will be delighted in how smoothly they are woven into some of the devotions, while those less familiar with them will still benefit from the content and strength of narrative flow.

The brief format of these Old Testament devotions allows you to read, mark, and inwardly digest God's Word whenever you have a few minutes. You can read these meditations to reset, reframe, rest, or even just think. No matter your intention, you will be blessed, receiving God's Word from the hand of the Trinity —from your heavenly Father, who creates and sustains the world,

His eternal Son, our Savior, and the Holy Spirit working through the Word and Word-made-Flesh. Thanks be to God!

Mary J. Moerbe is a wife, mother of six, deaconess (mercy worker) in the Lutheran Church—Missouri Synod, author, and speaker. Her publications include *Family Vocation: God's Calling in Marriage, Parenting, and Childhood*; *How Can I Help: God's Calling for Kids*; *Whisper, Whisper: Learning about Church*; and *Blessed: God's Gift of Love*. Her website, www.MaryJMoerbe.com, and her blog, "Meet, Write, and Salutary," encourage Lutherans to write and foster Lutheran community.

Introduction

*"Let the word of Christ dwell in you richly in all wisdom,
teaching and admonishing one another in psalms and hymns
and spiritual songs, singing with grace in your hearts
to the Lord." Colossians 3:16*

You don't need to read these meditations. Really! There is nothing here that you can't find in a devotion book written for any and all Christians. Women in general, and mothers in particular, have the same spiritual battles and needs as any other subset of human beings. Mothers, as well as wives, fathers, children, singles, the elderly, the rich, and the poor, need to be reminded of their sins, and we need to be pointed to the cross of Christ to find peace and forgiveness. Because there is both Law and Gospel in this book, there's really nothing that you can't find in another Bible-based devotion, or that you shouldn't receive regularly in the Divine Service. These meditations are certainly no substitute for a faithful pastor and the blessings of confession and absolution. If you choose to use these readings as daily devotional material, I pray they will be only one small part of your weekly exposure to the Word of God.

That being said, there are plenty of challenges unique to the vocation of motherhood. The meditations found in the following pages specifically hone in on God's comforting promises—to everyone, but also to mothers, who have so many others who need them night and day. As you read, I hope you find encouragement and solace as a mother, being reminded that God is working in you, through you, and also despite you. He keeps moms going when we feel we can't go on. In Christ, He forgives all of our failures and sends us the Holy Spirit to build us up for this work He has planned for us from eternity.

You don't have to be the "perfect" mom to read this; I'm not the perfect mom to write it! If you feel worried and concerned and burdened about mothering, then you're in the perfect position to be comforted by the message of the Gospel: Our perfect God sent His Son to take the punishment we deserve for our sins. You have been made right with God. Heaven is yours. Even though you will still struggle here on earth, your Father is with you, protecting and guiding each and every moment. He equips you for the vocation of motherhood, whether or not you feel adequate for the task.

I have few qualifications for writing a devotion book about motherhood. But, I have been blessed to be raised by Christian parents from infancy. I attended Lutheran schools for my entire education, especially enjoying classes at Bethany Lutheran College entitled *Teaching the Christian Faith* and *Hymnody and Liturgics.* I've also spent much of my mothering career as a La Leche League leader, learning the intimate reflections and thoughts of mothers who are struggling to find their way. I myself am an insecure, sinful mom of six who needs constant reminding of God's love and forgiveness in Christ. If for no other reason than that, God has equipped me to write for you from my own inadequacies and the comfort I've received from reading His Word.

I write not only as a Christian, but specifically as a Lutheran, and I pray that those doctrines are thoroughly embedded in these meditations. For those who are not familiar with Confessional Lutheranism, four things set it apart from other denominations:

1) *Law and Gospel.* Our churches teach a distinction between Law and Gospel as found in the Bible. The Law is found in Scripture when believers are told what they must do, or what they haven't done correctly. It shows us that we cannot save ourselves and are lost in our own sin. The Law also gives the forgiven Christian directions on how to serve God and our neighbors. The Gospel is found in Scripture when we are told of our Savior, Jesus, and how He takes away our sins and makes us right with God because of His death and resurrection. Both the teachings of Law and Gospel are found in the Bible and both must be taught, but the Gospel should always predominate because only Christ, and never our works, can save.

2) *The Means of Grace.* Lutherans believe in the Means of Grace, in Word and Sacrament. God works faith in people through

His Word, the Bible, but also through the actions that Jesus instituted for His Church. The Holy Spirit brings faith when we hear the Word of God, and also by baptism and the Lord's Supper. He actually strengthens His Church through these means, rather than providing them simply as symbols. Lutherans focus on the Means of Grace as the main ways through which God works in the hearts of believers.

3) *Luther's Small Catechism*. Our main doctrines can be found in the six chief parts of the Small Catechism, a summary of the teachings of the Bible compiled by Martin Luther. These six parts give a concise language for Lutherans, which we all memorize prior to being admitted to the Lord's Supper. They are The Ten Commandments, The Apostle's Creed, The Lord's Prayer, Baptism, The Lord's Supper, and The Office of the Keys. Please read them in their entirety, with meanings, in Appendix 1.

4) *The Doctrine of Vocation*. The Doctrine of Vocation is the teaching from the Bible that God channels His blessing through the service of individuals. Vocation is *not* what line of work you choose, but rather, what you are already doing. It means if God has given you children, then He means for you to be a mother, and through this vocation, He will provide for and bless your babies. It means you don't have to sell your possessions and become a missionary in order to do God's work. You don't need to go searching for God's calling. His work is being done through you, all around you, as you serve those in your midst.

While many Christians agree with the preceding points, Lutherans give them distinctive emphasis, and I want my readers to understand that I write from such a perspective. However, whether you are Lutheran or not, you still have much to gain as a Christian mom from these reflections. You'll find that Lutherans and your denomination have a lot in common—conservative Lutherans truly believe Scripture is the inspired Word of God and hold it in high regard. These meditations are each based on a passage of Scripture, with encouragement to read the passage in context in your own Bible. References to the Catechism can be looked up in Appendix 1, which is a translation of Martin Luther's summary of the important teachings of the Bible, including many

teachings that are broadly shared among various Christian
denominations. I hope, therefore, that any Christian mom can feel
"at home" with these meditations. You'll also find beautiful, time-
tested hymns, full of rich theology, which can be appreciated and
treasured by any Christian.

One of my overarching goals in writing this book is to clearly
present the Law and the Gospel in the context of motherhood.
Most of the individual devotions do just that. However, a few of
them are more reflective or instructive in nature, based on 2
Timothy 3:16, "All Scripture is...useful for teaching...and training
in righteousness, that the [Christian] may be complete,
thoroughly equipped for every good work," like the daily toils and
joys of motherhood. Many of the meditations focus specifically on
the redemptive work of Christ; others emphasize the providential
care of God the Father, or the sanctifying power of the Holy Spirit.
Whatever the spotlight, every meditation is harmonious with the
Gospel, many of them referencing the forgiveness received when
we partake of the Lord's Supper or were baptized.

It was an interesting process to choose which passages to
include in this book of meditations. Reading through several
chapters of the Old Testament in a single sitting was fascinating,
giving me a long-term perspective and a big-picture context of
how the various parts of the Old Testament form a cohesive
whole. As I read, I noted passages that pertained to my role as a
mother, and later wrote reflections on those Scripture readings. I
wanted to include at least one devotion from each of the 39 books
in order to give the reader some familiarity with the lesser known
books, and also arrange them in roughly chronological order
(though much of the time-line is up for debate). When a
meditation is based on a lesser-known book, or is placed in a
potentially unexpected spot, it includes a few sentences of
introduction for clarity. Finally, I found that matching hymns to
the Scripture readings was inspirational and edifying. There are
no formal prayers in this book; you'll find a rich treasury of
thoughtful prayers in your own hymnal or prayer books that you
may use at the end of each meditation. Or feel free to compose
your own heartfelt prayers.

I gathered many of the historical and theological notes from The People's Bible Commentary Series and the Zondervan NIV Study Bible. Strong's Concordance was also invaluable for studying Hebrew words.

May God richly bless you as you endeavor to do His will, serving your children to His glory and honor.

In Christ,

Marie

P.S. If you have suggestions or ideas for either the next edition of this book or the upcoming *Volume 2: New Testament*, you are welcome to contact me:

www.intoyourhandsllc.com/contact

Notes:

All hymns are taken from the *Evangelical Lutheran Hymnary*, 1996. They are used by permission and can be found at https://hymnary.org/hymnal/ELH1996. If you would like to find these hymns in a hymnal other than the *ELH*, please see the conversion chart in Appendix 2.

Bible passages are from the New King James Version, unless otherwise noted. They are used by permission.

The photos of the hands on the front cover symbolize how God uses the hands of mothers as His instruments.

S.D.G.

Pain, in Childbirth and More

"To the woman [God] said: 'I will greatly multiply your sorrow and your conception; In pain you shall bring forth children.'"
Genesis 3:16

Some folks say that as soon as you have your baby in your arms, you forget the pain of childbirth. I'm not so sure. I technically can't recall the intensity of the "ring of fire," but I know the births of my children have been the most excruciating pain I've ever experienced, yes—even the one with the epidural! Even beyond the difficulty of labor and delivery, motherhood is full of bumps, bruises, jabs, and whacks as our children try to show affection to us and to one another. We just can't get around the fact that pain is part of our humble existence after the Fall into Sin.

But pain isn't our eternal destiny. In fact, in the verse immediately prior to the woman's curse of pain in childbirth, God gave Adam and Eve the promise of a Savior. Christ experienced pain for us—more pain than we'll ever have to experience, thanks be to God! Jesus not only lived a perfect life of obedience to His heavenly Father in your place, He was whipped, tortured, and finally gave His dying breath on the cross, all because He loves you! Another 3:16 reference in the Bible gives us the Gospel in the nutshell: "For God so loved the world that He gave His only begotten Son, that whoever believes in Him should not perish but have everlasting life" (John 3:16). In place of the pain we experience in this world, God promises us the gift of heaven, where there will be no more weeping or crying or pain (Rev. 21:4).

When through fiery trials your pathway shall lie,
My grace, all-sufficient, shall be your supply.
The flame shall not hurt you; My only design:
Your dross to consume and your gold to refine. (521:4)

For Further Reading: Genesis 3; Revelation 21

Who Can Rob Me of Heaven?

"'Naked I came from my mother's womb, And naked shall I return there. The Lord gave, and the Lord has taken away; Blessed be the name of the Lord....Shall we indeed accept good from God, and shall we not accept adversity?' In all this Job did not sin with his lips." Job 1:21–22; 2:10

Many scholars believe that the Book of Job may have been the first Scriptures written down. It is thought to be set around the time of Abraham—Job is his own family's priest (1:5), like Abraham. Perhaps it takes place shortly after the time of Noah, with the Ice Age still remaining (37:6–10) due to the catastrophic conditions of the flood in an otherwise arid climate.

The Book of Job commences with Satan appearing before God, accusing Job of faithfulness to God only because of material blessings and good health. God gives Satan permission to withdraw these gifts from Job. His wealth is taken, his children are killed, and his health deteriorates to the point that he wishes he were dead. Thus Job's faith is tested.

Hopefully no reader is experiencing loss to the same extent as Job, but we all experience troubles and loss. As children of God, what else is there to say, but the words of Job? Just like Job, we know our struggles are not a punishment for sin, but rather a trial that will end in spiritual blessing. Your earthly struggles may remain, but be assured that God has already punished your sins in Christ. Heaven is your sure destination after grief is over!

Why should cross and trial grieve me?
Christ is near With His cheer; Never will He leave me.
Who can rob me of the heaven
That God's Son For my own To my faith hath given?
God oft gives me days of gladness;
Shall I grieve If He give Seasons, too, of sadness?
God is good and tempers ever
All my ill, And He will Wholly leave me never. (377:1,3)

For Further Reading: Job 1 and 2; Romans 8:1–11

Higher

"Can you search out the deep things of God? Can you find out the limits of the Almighty? They are higher than heaven—what can you do? Deeper than Sheol [the grave]—what can you know? Their measure is longer than the earth And broader than the sea." Job 11:7–9

The Book of Job continues with the main character's three friends attempting to teach or comfort him. In a series of speeches, these friends share their admonitions for Job—urging him to repent of his sins. Job alternates replies, clearing his name and defending his actions. In the passage above, his friend Zophar endeavors to comfort Job, stating that as mere humans, there's no way we can expect to know the mind of God.

The prophet Isaiah mirrors a similar sentiment, but in the words of God Himself: "For my thoughts are not your thoughts, neither are your ways my ways....For as the heavens are higher than the earth, so are my ways higher than your ways and my thoughts than your thoughts." He goes on to remind His children that His Word is powerful and life-changing, even if the results are not immediately noticeable.

So it is with motherhood. God's ways are higher than our own. For many of us, being a mother doesn't bring the joy or fulfillment we imagined it would. There are disappointments and crosses to bear. We struggle as we face our own inadequacies. But that doesn't mean this journey isn't worth it! God made you into a mother; He will provide for you every step of the way. And sometimes, though we may not understand when or how, our greatest fears are used as blessings from God to bring us closer to Christ and His never-ending, unstoppable, grave-denying love.

Ye fearful saints, fresh courage take; The clouds ye so much dread Are big with mercy and shall break In blessings on your head. Judge not the Lord by feeble sense, But trust Him for His grace; Behind a frowning providence He hides a smiling face. (434:2)

For Further Reading: Job 11; Isaiah 55:8–11

Unconditional Trust

"Though He slay me, yet will I trust Him." Job 13:15

Spoiler alert! God does *not* kill Job, and in fact, blesses him abundantly beyond his losses in the end! What an advantage we have as readers, knowing his whole story from beginning to end! Poor Job, at the time, had no idea how his life would turn out. He grieved his great losses and wanted vindication before the Lord.

During the course of his troubles, Job himself admits that he isn't patient (6:11, 21:4). However, he does persevere under trial. Before he knows "the rest of the story," Job boldly declares that even if God would kill him, he trusts Him. In this passage, the Hebrew word used for "trust" can also mean "to hope for; to wait for; to expect." Job knew that, in the end, God would make everything right.

As you experience life's trials, before you know how your story will turn out, wait on the Lord and hope in Him. All Hell could break loose in your life—and who hasn't had a moment like that?—and yet, Jesus reigns for your absolute good. He went through the ultimate trial and persevered on your behalf. Therefore, we can face our difficulties in life with perseverance, considering them pure joy. James 1:12 reminds us that "Blessed is the one who perseveres under trial because, having stood the test, that person will receive the crown of life that the Lord has promised to those who love him" (NIV).

> *In Thine arms I rest me;*
> *Foes who would molest me*
> *Cannot reach me here.*
> *Though the earth be shaking,*
> *Ev'ry heart be quaking,*
> *Jesus calms my fear.*
> *Lightnings flash And thunders crash;*
> *Yet, though sin and hell assail me,*
> *Jesus will not fail me. (263:2)*

For Further Reading: Job 13; James 1 and 5:11

Blessed, to Be a Blessing

"In you all the families of the earth shall be blessed."
Genesis 12:3

In the Scripture passage above, God is speaking to Abram. He commands him to leave his country, and promises to bless the world through his descendants, and namely, the Descendant, Christ. Here, God is once again repeating the promise of a Savior that He first gave in Genesis 3. Our gracious Father in Heaven foreshadows the first coming of Abram's greatest Son, Jesus.

Though the promise above is given in a specific context, it is also true for each and every Christian mother. Whether your children are begotten or adopted, through them, God blesses the world. The first coming of Christ has passed, but while we wait for His second coming, there is work to do. Sometimes as mothers, we might feel hindered from doing the Lord's work, as if our domestic work were a distraction from God's true callings. But raising our children in the faith *is* God's calling! As mothers, we remind our kids that the Holy Ghost daily and richly forgives us and all believers all our sins. God can touch exponentially more people with the message of His love through all of them than just through you! When the Holy Spirit has worked in their hearts, they (and their children and their children's children) can evangelize the lost long after you have entered your eternal rest. You have been blessed by God to be a blessing to your children, and through your children, a blessing to the world.

> *Make them apostles,*
> *Heralds of Thy cross;*
> *Forth may they go to tell all realms Thy grace.*
> *Inspired of Thee,*
> *May they count all but loss*
> *And stand at last with joy before Thy face. (501:5)*

For Further Reading: Genesis 12; Acts 7:1–8

Company on the Journey

"Then Jacob made a vow, saying, 'If God will be with me, and keep me in this way that I am going, and give me bread to eat and clothing to put on, so that I come back to my father's house in peace, then the Lord shall be my God.'" Genesis 28:20–21

Motherhood starts in an instant, but it certainly becomes a journey quickly. While the journey of motherhood takes us women on a twisting turning road—stretching our hearts to love the little people among us more and more—it also quickly teaches us our own faults and inadequacies, and the need for our merciful Father in Heaven.

When Jacob made the vow in the passage above, he also was on a journey, going to Haran to take shelter from his vengeful brother Esau. He promised to serve God, trusting that God would provide for his safety and needs. God doesn't need to prove Himself to you. Through the death and resurrection of His Son, God has already secured your eternal safety, and through His providence, He richly and daily gives all the material possessions our families need.

While on this journey, take comfort that the Lord will never leave you nor forsake you (Hebrews 13:5) because you are His own dear child, bought at a great price. And just as the Lord safely returned Jacob to his fatherland after many years, so also the Lord will take you, His own redeemed child, to your homeland in Heaven. Is this journey of motherhood easy? No, but we've got Almighty Company the whole way!

> *I walk with Jesus all the way;*
> *His guidance never fails me.*
> *Within His wounds I find a stay*
> *When Satan's pow'r assails me,*
> *And, by His footsteps led, My path I safely tread.*
> *In spite of ills that threaten may,*
> *I walk with Jesus all the way. (252:5)*

For Further Reading: Genesis 28–32; Psalm 105:8–15

Wrestling for a Blessing

*"[Jacob] said [to God], 'I will not let You go
unless You bless me!'" Genesis 32:26*

None of us has ever physically wrestled with God, as Jacob did in the Scripture passage above. But, if you're anything like me, you've wrestled with Him spiritually. We wrestle with disappointments: why can't my family be...? why won't this child learn to...? when will I get to...? We wrestle with sins: when will I be more...? why can't I stop...? how will we make it through...? We wrestle with failure: why did I...? why can't I...? when will I learn to...?

God gives you permission to wrestle with Him in prayer. He promises to hear our prayers (1 John 5:14). We can ask Him anything "with all boldness and confidence, as children ask their dear father." We cannot demand that God do whatever we ask like a magic genie, but we can hold Him to the promises He gives us in His Word: He forgives us our sins. He gives us new life in the Spirit. He promises that all things work together for the good of those who love Him (Romans 8:28). Don't be afraid to wrestle with God as Jacob did. "Call upon Him in every trouble, pray, praise, and give thanks."

*Call on God, knock, seek, implore Him,
'Tis the Christian's noblest skill;
He who comes with faith before Him
Meets with help and favor still:
Who on God most firmly rest
Are the wisest and the best;
God will with such strength imbue them,
Ne'er shall any foe subdue them. (256:3)*

For Further Reading: Genesis 32; Luke 11:9–13

The Lord Prospers You

"The Lord was with [Joseph]; and whatever he did, the Lord made it prosper." Genesis 39:23

Joseph had just been propositioned by Potiphar's wife and turned her down. But she flipped the story inside out and lied that *he* had tried to sleep with her! He lost his job (slave though he may have been) and was thrown into prison. How's that for a bad day? And yet, Scripture says that the Lord was with Joseph.

Hopefully none of us feels like our homes are a prison, and our children are the jail guards, but let's admit it: sometimes, we do feel boxed in and trapped. The work is never-ending. There are always more clothes to fold, more dishes to wash, more homework to check over, and more tummies to feed, not to mention the fights to be broken up that always abound!

But, the Lord has called you to your position. If God can mold Joseph's life into a grand plan while he's in the clinker, He can surely prosper you, as well. We're not necessarily talking about material wealth or riches here, though! Nowhere in the Bible does God promise you earthly health, wealth, or happiness. However, He does promise a deep and fulfilling joy to His children: the peace that surpasses understanding through Christ Jesus (Philippians 4:7). This peace belongs to you as a mother, and through you, to your children. That's true prosperity, no matter our life's circumstances!

> *Help me, for I am weak; I fight,*
> *Yet scarce can battle longer.*
> *I cling but to Thy grace and might,*
> *'Tis Thou must make me stronger.*
> *When sore temptations are my lot,*
> *And tempests round me lower, Break their power;*
> *So through deliv'rance wrought,*
> *I know that Thou forsak'st me not! (255:5)*

For Further Reading: Genesis 39; Psalm 105:16–22; Acts 7:9–16

Lavish Grace

"Pharaoh's daughter said to [Moses' mother], 'Take this child away and nurse him for me, and I will give you your wages.' So the woman took the child and nursed him." Exodus 2:9

Every mother has protective instincts to some extent, but think of how Moses' mother Jochebed's adrenaline must have been pumping! All of the Hebrew baby boys were to be drowned in the Nile river, according to the decree of the Pharaoh. But Jochebed kept her precious son hidden for three months until it became too dangerous to continue to hide him. The basket into which she placed him floated on the river, and ended up being Moses' salvation when he was found by the Egyptian princess, and later raised by her.

Our society currently enjoys vastly greater freedom than the Israelites did under the tyranny of the Egyptians. But, we as mothers still want to protect our children from the devastating spiritual effects of sin, death, and the power of the devil. Our good Lord rescues our children—not with a pitch-coated basket floating down the river, but in the saving waters of baptism. In Jochebed's case, God not only spared her son's life to His glory, He also poured grace upon grace by allowing Jochebed to care for, teach, and nurse her infant son. Today, God has not only our spiritual needs in mind, He also lavishes us daily with earthly blessings, even on the rough days. He gives us little lives who forgive us for our failures. What lavish grace that the Lord not only helps us to recall our baptism and die daily to our flesh, but also to recall His providence, and rise daily to raise our children for Him.

For the joy Thy birth doth give me, For Thy holy, precious Word;
For Thy Baptism which doth save me,
For Thy blest Communion board;
For Thy death, the bitter scorn, For Thy resurrection morn,
Lord, I thank Thee and extol Thee,
And in heav'n I shall behold Thee. (354:10)

For Further Reading: Exodus 2; Acts 7:20–29; 1 Peter 3:21

Surrender Your Disappointments

"So the Lord said to [Moses], 'Who has made man's mouth? Or who makes the mute, the deaf, the seeing, or the blind? Have not I, the Lord? Now therefore, go, and I will be with your mouth and teach you what you shall say.'" Exodus 4:11–12

Rarely is life picture-perfect. As a mother, I have found myself occasionally surprised that my children's health is not how I planned, either. None of my children have major disabilities or life-threatening illnesses, but we have had physical challenges, nonetheless. Sometimes when grappling with these difficulties, it can be easy to wonder why God hasn't intervened to fix everything.

Yes, our family's physical challenges—whether they be sickness, handicaps, or otherwise—are a result of sin in a fallen world. But that doesn't mean God isn't in control. In the verse above, God takes credit for His creation, disabilities and all. God doesn't make mistakes, and He can and will use us and our children for His glory, just like He used Moses (speech disorder and all!) to accomplish some amazing things! Sometimes, His purposes are hidden, and often, we won't ever understand these limitations in this lifetime. But dwelling in disappointment won't help us. Continue to ask, seek, and knock (Mt. 7:7–8). Pray that the Lord will open your heart to surrender to His will and seek His glory in physical challenges. Our own Savior took on human flesh Himself, with all of its humiliation, in order that we may be exalted with Him in the bodily resurrection to come.

> *If our blessed Lord and Maker*
> *Hated men,*
> *Would He then*
> *Be of flesh partaker?*
> *If He in our woe delighted,*
> *Would He bear*
> *All the care*
> *Of our race benighted? (115:5)*

For Further Reading: Exodus 4; Acts 7:30–35; John 9:1–5

Conversational Mentoring

"So it shall be, when your son asks you in time to come, saying, 'What is this?' that you shall say to him, 'By strength of hand the Lord brought us out of Egypt, out of the house of bondage.'"
Exodus 13:14

Whatever the reason, kids don't always get their chores done and Mom has to pick up the pieces. This happened to me recently, and it reminded me of how much the work is divided among our family members in order to share meals together. Do you ever get tired of cooking, washing the dishes afterward, wiping the sticky mess off of the table, sweeping the floor, or constantly prompting your children to do so? And once it's done, you have to do it all over again! All of the preparation, execution, and clean-up can be exhausting.

But, it's worth it. In the passage above, Moses is instructing the Israelites in "table conversation" for the Passover meal. Part of the reason behind having this family celebration together was for the education that took place. The Israelites were instructed to tell the story of their salvation from Egypt each year. Having your own family gather around your table sets a regular time for family prayer and Bible readings to grow in our knowledge of salvation. Even when we aren't specifically having a devotion at mealtime, we can season our conversation with Godly salt. This is a wonderful time to share with our children our thanks to God for his goodness, and praise Him together for His Son, our Savior. Meals together can be difficult, but stay the course! Use this time to mentor your children in the faith by the Holy Spirit.

Taught to lisp the holy praises
Which on earth Thy children sing,
Both with lips and hearts unfeignéd,
May we our thank-off'rings bring,
Then with all the saints in glory
Join to praise our Lord and King. (367:5)

For Further Reading: Exodus 13; Deut. 6:20-25; Psalm 78:1–16

Dry Feet

"You in Your mercy have led forth The people whom You have redeemed; You have guided them in Your strength To Your holy habitation." Exodus 15:13

When we refer to Biblical poetry, the Book of Psalms usually comes to mind, not Exodus. But this passage is taken from the Song of Moses, right after God had delivered His people from the Egyptians at the Red Sea.

Blocked on every side, the Hebrew people lost all hope. At first, they had been thrilled with freedom from Egypt, but their joy turned to sadness, trapped at the Red Sea by Pharaoh's pursuing army. But the Lord had not left them. In fact, He defended His people as a pillar of cloud and divided the enemy from them. He orchestrated events so His pursued people could pass through the Red Sea on dry land. Thus Pharaoh's mighty army perished in the Sea, and drowned were the king's ambitions of re-enslavement.

Do you ever feel blocked at every side? No matter how you try to plan, prepare, or solve your family's problems, obstacles arise? Don't lose hope! Don't let Satan, the master of Pharaoh, steal your joy and turn it into sadness. God will part the troubled waters for you. It might not be on your desired time-line, but you can always trust the Parter-of-Waters to stand between you and your problems as a pillar of cloud until the time is right to open up an unmuddied path. Christ has already brought you through the greatest trouble of your sins, and He will surely remain with you through any earthly obstacle. Look! Your feet are dry.

> *Come, ye faithful, raise the strain Of triumphant gladness!*
> *God hath brought His Israel*
> *Into joy from sadness.*
> *Loosed from Pharaoh's bitter yoke Jacob's sons and daughters,*
> *Led them with unmoistened foot*
> *Through the Red Sea waters. (347:1)*

For Further Reading: Exodus 15; Acts 7:36; 1 Corinthians 10:1–4

Manna Provided

"I have heard the complaints of the children of Israel. Speak to them, saying, 'At twilight you shall eat meat, and in the morning you shall be filled with bread. And you shall know that I am the Lord your God.'" Exodus 16:12

How easy it is to be like the Hebrews, complaining about food. Shopping for food. Cooking food. Baking food. Packing food. Eating food (cold). And let's just say...wiping the bottoms that process that food!

It's certainly easy to worry about food, too. We confess in the meaning to the Fourth Petition, "God certainly gives daily bread without our prayer, even to all the wicked; but we pray...that He would lead us to acknowledge this and to receive our daily bread with thanksgiving." In our hearts, we know God will give our Christian families (and even the heathen!) all that we need; we *shouldn't* worry. Yet, the planner in us still wants to take control!

Our Lord is a worker of miracles. Just as He provided manna in the wilderness, He'll provide us with daily bread. He can even wipe away our worries. Let's ask the Holy Spirit to create in us a sanctified habit: Rather than complain about lack as the Israelites did, or worry about tomorrow's food, we instead pour out our needs before our Heavenly Father in prayer, acknowledging His goodness in feeding our families daily, and most importantly, with the Bread of Life.

> *Round each habitation hov'ring,*
> *See the cloud and fire appear,*
> *For a glory and a cov'ring,*
> *Showing that the Lord is near.*
> *Thus they march, the pillar leading,*
> *Light by night and shade by day,*
> *Daily on the manna feeding*
> *Which He gives them when they pray. (214:3)*

For Further Reading: Exodus 16; Ps. 78:17–29; Matthew 6:31–34

Holding Up Hands

"But Moses' hands became heavy....And Aaron and Hur
supported his hands, one on one side, and the other
on the other side." Exodus 17:12

It's a familiar Sunday School lesson. Moses and friends were on a hill to watch Joshua and the Israelites fight against the Amalekites. When Moses' hands were up, the Israelites gained the advantage; when he rested, they started to lose. Moses' helpers physically lifted up his hands for the win. God's prophets all need support. And there's a time and place to be the giver of that help.

Whose hands do you hold up? Often the world views a person's worth only by a paying job. During your years of motherhood, you might not be paid a cent! Perhaps you're so burnt out caring for little ones, you can't even manage a volunteer position in your church or community. Maybe you feel like a failure because you are not "holding up" the hands of an important missionary or spiritual leader. Mother, don't fret. God has given you your children and this season of life. They may not be big or important to the world, but your children are important to God! Daily, as you hold (up) their hands, you are fulfilling God's calling, shepherding members of His church. You can also teach kids the importance of praying for their pastor(s), who regularly teach them of Jesus' dying love. Fold your hands around their little hands, making intercession for our modern prophets.

If you cannot speak like angels, If you cannot preach like Paul,
You can tell the love of Jesus; You can say He died for all.
If you cannot rouse the wicked With the Judgment's dread alarms,
You can lead the little children To the Savior's waiting arms.
If you cannot be a watchman, Standing high on Zion's wall,
Pointing out the path to heaven, Off'ring life and peace to all,
With your prayers and with your off'rings
You can do what God demands;
You can be like faithful Aaron, Holding up the prophet's hands.
(191:2,3)

For Further Reading: Exodus 17; 1 Timothy 2:1

Mercifully Adopted

"I, the Lord your God, am a jealous God, visiting the iniquity of the fathers upon the children to the third and fourth generations of those who hate Me, but showing mercy to thousands, to those who love Me and keep My commandments." Exodus 20:5–6

I love that this passage expresses the intergenerational importance of passing down God's Word to our children and grandchildren. It isn't enough to hope our children understand; we want to immerse them in God's love and be sure they are prepared to teach these truths to their own children, and their grandchildren after that!

It's a big responsibility, isn't it? In fact, it's an overwhelming burden for us to know that God will "visit our iniquity" to our grandchildren and great-grandchildren, especially when evil is the favorite pastime of our sinful nature. In light of this passage, we might ask ourselves, "Have I kept God's commandments *well enough* that He will show mercy to the generations after me?"

Keep in mind, though, that keeping God's commandments is law. We will *never* fulfill them perfectly. That's why Jesus came to wash away our sins and make us right with God. He has adopted us into God's family, fully and freely, without any merit or worthiness in us. Clinging to Christ for the unmerited forgiveness of our sins, the Holy Spirit changes us into new creatures, adopting us into God's family, regardless of past sins. "For Christ is the end of the law...to everyone who believes" (Rom. 10:4), including you, your children, and generations yet to come.

> *Moses' law no longer rules us,*
> *Christ's free Spirit gently schools us;*
> *Ended now our captive thrall;*
> *He who heeds God's gracious call,*
> *Through his Savior's death and merit,*
> *Now enjoys adoption's spirit;*
> *Alleluia! Alleluia! (95:6)*

For Further Reading: Exodus 20; Eph. 1:4-6; Heb. 12:18–24

A Tiny Nation Redeemed

*"Show me now Your way, that I may know You and that I may
find grace in Your sight. And consider that this nation
is Your people." Exodus 33:13*

In the context of this passage, God has just given the Ten
Commandments, broken up the idolatrous worship of a golden
calf, and commanded that the Israelites depart from Mt. Sinai
toward the Promised Land. Moses has been through a lot of
drama in a few short months! He begs the Lord to go with him to
direct his path, both physically and spiritually.

I'll bet you have drama in your life, too. Maybe not to the
same degree as the Hebrew nation, but still! We pray with the
psalmist, "Show me Your ways, O Lord; Teach me Your paths.
Lead me in Your truth and teach me, for You are the God of my
salvation" (Psalm 25:4–5). If the Lord doesn't direct our paths, we
have no hope. But He does! Even when struggles or decisions lie
in front of you, you remain a baptized child of God through it all.
You and your family are a dearly bought people of God, even as
Israel was in the Old Testament. If God would fight for that nation
and lead them, He will certainly not forget you and your tiny
nation in your time of trouble! He has purchased you with the
blood of His Son, Jesus, and washed you clean in the waters of
baptism. Heaven is your home!

---

*He that believes and is baptized
Shall see the Lord's salvation;
Baptized into the death of Christ,
He is a new creation.
Through Christ's redemption he shall stand
Among the glorious heav'nly band
Of ev'ry tribe and nation. (241:1)*

For Further Reading: Exodus 33; Psalm 25; Acts 7:38–43

Pardon for the Stiff-Necked

"Let my Lord, I pray, go among us, even though we are a stiff-necked people; and pardon our iniquity and our sin."
Exodus 34:9

Are your offspring stubborn? Maybe a certain child in particular comes to mind. When we've explained this concept to our children as they struggle, we've equated stubbornness with the Biblical idea of being "stiff-necked." The problem is, it isn't just the children who struggle!

It is easy for us as mothers to be stubborn as well, especially when we try to justify it for the "right" reason of exacting obedience from our children. Stubbornness means not bending one's heart, just as being stiff-necked means not bending one's head. In the text above, Moses was pleading for his people before God, and God chooses to renew His covenant of grace. After violation by the opposing side, any earthly party would have annulled the contract; God, however, obligated Himself to keep His covenant with Abraham's descendants, even after they had rebelled against Him. It was God's free choice to continue to pardon them; He renewed His covenant as only He could. Our Lord and Savior didn't have to choose us, either. He has made our scarlet stubbornness as white as snow. The Holy Spirit bends our stubborn hearts to show His agape love and mercy to our children, and in turn to forgive them when they are stubborn, just as we have been forgiven. What precious good news to know our necks aren't permanently stiff!

Then on Him I cast my burden,
Sink it in the depth below.
Let me know Thy gracious pardon;
Wash me, make me white as snow.
Let Thy Spirit leave me never;
Make me only Thine forever. (450:4)

For Further Reading: Exodus 34; Micah 7:14–20; Acts 7:51–60

Fire and Ice

"You shall not take vengeance, nor bear any grudge against the children of your people, but you shall love your neighbor as yourself: I am the Lord." Leviticus 19:18

Kids. They can be so headstrong, can't they?! They erupt in anger so easily. They pout and whine when they don't get their way. In fact, they are a lot like their mothers. Often, we soothe our consciences, saying that we are correct, our way is better, or we've got their best in mind. But truly, we moms have moments when our hearts are just as icy as our children's.

In the passage above, God reminds us that He is the Lord. If anyone has a "right" to demand His own way, it's the Creator of the Universe, the Maker of Heaven and Earth. God requires in His law that we not bear any grudges. Christian moms can especially see our failure in this regard when we look into the mirror of the law. We are filthy. We "forgive" in lip-service to our children, but in our hearts we count their sins against them and let their injuries affect our interactions with them in the future. God demands perfection. But where God demands, He also provides.

Our Savior Jesus bore no grudges of His own. The only grudges He bore were ours: those He took with Him to destroy at the cross. When we reflect on Jesus' fiery passion and His warm love toward us that led Him to a bitter, searing death, God melts our icy hearts. He gives us strength to forgive the wounds our children generate, not just with our words, but also with our hearts. He has forgiven us fully and loves us as His own self, yes—even as His dearly loved children.

> *Exalt our low desires,*
> *Extinguish passion's fires,*
> *Heal ev'ry wound.*
> *Our stubborn spirits bend,*
> *Our icy coldness end, Our devious steps attend*
> *While heav'nward bound. (11:4)*

For Further Reading: Leviticus 19; Ephesians 4:32

Good Intentions

*"Moses, Aaron, and the whole Israelite community did with the
Levites just as the Lord commanded Moses."*
Numbers 8:20 (NIV)

The last two-plus books of the Bible previous to this Scripture
reference have set forth hundreds of rules and regulations, not
only for the construction of the Tabernacle, but also for the proper
worship of Yahweh. When presented with these details, both large
and small, the Israelites promised their obedience and set to
work.

And they did well. For a while. But after further study of
Hebrew history, we know that Israel's allegiance to the One True
God swayed. They did as the Lord commanded, but only at first.

We often have the same problem. We make resolutions (to
yell less, be more patient, stop checking Facebook so often, etc.).
We may do well for a while—weeks, days, moments—but we so
often fall back into our old habits. A similar pattern is evident in
our offspring. Our desires and our actions are often at odds.

Thank God that He redeems our actions. We know our own
obedience is so paltry that it could never be good enough for God.
In the meaning of the Fifth Petition, we pray that God "would give
us everything by grace, for we daily sin much and deserve nothing
but punishment." And we remember God's mercy to us as we deal
with our children: "We on our part will heartily forgive and
readily do good to those who sin against us."

The task Thy wisdom hath assigned,
O let me cheerfully fulfill;
In all my works Thy presence find,
And prove Thy good and perfect will.
Thee may I set at my right hand,
Whose eyes my inmost substance see,
And labor on at Thy command,
And offer all my works to Thee. (506:2,3)

For Further Reading: Numbers 8; Psalm 136

Long Arms

"[Moses said,] 'I cannot carry all these people by myself; the burden is too heavy for me....The Lord answered Moses, 'Is the Lord's arm too short?'" Numbers 11:14,23 (NIV)

The people were fussing again. They were complaining about their food. And they came to Moses to do their whining. Ever feel like Moses?

Moses pours out his heart to God. He just can't take it anymore. The constant complaining! The never-ending bottomless bellies. The hoards of people Moses is supposed to feed! At this point, Moses is so desperate that he even prefers death to the continuation of his calling! He just can't do the job that God has called him to do. Maybe you feel even more like Moses now.

How does the Lord answer Moses? How does the Lord answer you? "Is the Lord's arm too short?" The Lord's arm, which fought for Israel against the Egyptians, will also fight against the peril of want in the wilderness. The hand at the end of the arm will pour out sustenance so abundantly to His people that there would be *too much* quail! Do not think that the Lord's arm is too short for you today. He can equip you to have "long arms" to meet the needs of those in your care.

Some days do seem like a battle, whether the battle is against those in our family and their complaints, or the devil, the world, and our own sinful flesh. But the Lord's arm is never too short. He has purchased you, His precious child, with His very blood, spreading His arms for you upon the cross. Those same arms are strong to do battle for you, whatever your struggles in life.

Amen, Lord Jesus, grant our prayer;
Great Captain, now Thine arm make bare,
Fight for us once again!
So shall Thy saints and martyrs raise
A mighty chorus to Thy praise,
World without end. Amen. (375:4)

For Further Reading: Numbers 11; Isaiah 59:1; Luke 1:51

Strange Words

"So the donkey said to Balaam, 'Am I not your donkey on which you have ridden, ever since I became yours, to this day? Was I ever disposed to do this to you?'" Numbers 22:30

Isn't it sometimes funny the words that come out of your mouth as a mother? "I've told you a hundred times: Take that asparagus out of the hamster ball and stop rubbing it on the window!" There are some strange words in Scripture, too. When Balaam's donkey speaks, it's surprising to me that the Bible doesn't point out how odd it is for a donkey to speak. No speech or preface. No parenthetical reference. God performed a miracle, and that's that.

There are some strange and unexpected words, precious words, that I hear every week in church. After I confess my sinfulness, my pastor assures me of God's forgiveness: "In the stead and by the command of our Lord Jesus Christ I forgive you all your sins, in the name of the Father and of the Son and of the Holy Spirit. Amen." How can this be? I inherited sin from my parents, and have given it to my children. I choose to "follow my heart" and commit sin. I speak and act selfishly. I am depraved and separated from the Holy Judge through my own fault. But, the God of the universe made a way to bring us together again. He brought forth His Son, born of a virgin: God-made-man for us. Jesus was nailed to the cross and died, speaking unthinkable words for a God-man, "It is finished." Jesus has paid the price for all of our mistakes. Strange, blessed words, indeed.

Precious Jesus, I beseech Thee,
May Thy words take root in me;
May this gift from heav'n enrich me
So that I bear fruit for Thee!
Take them never from my heart
Till I see Thee as Thou art,
When in heav'nly bliss and glory
I shall greet Thee and adore Thee. (230:4)

For Further Reading: Numbers 22; John 20:19–23

Up!

"In the wilderness...you saw how the Lord your God carried you, as a man carries his son, in all the way that you went until you came to this place." Deuteronomy 1:31

I love to babywear! It seems that little ones constantly want "up!" A sling or a carrier allows me to snuggle a child, give him or her a view, and get things done all at the same time. The child feels safe and secure, and if you're lucky, might even fall asleep on the ride. But if you've ever done babywearing, you know it doesn't always work...like if you're eight months pregnant, or if you have a pulled shoulder muscle, or if a specific child doesn't have the personality to enjoy the ride.

Thank God that He never tires of carrying His children! Are you tired, dear mother? Anxious? Second-guessing your choices? Cast your burden on the Lord, and He will sustain you (Ps. 55:22)! In fact, He's carrying you already, like a sheep on His shoulder. That love you have for your children, pales in comparison to His love for you! He's never too exhausted to continue to care for you, nor to strengthen you for the care you give others.

Jesus has carried all of your anxieties and weariness to the cross. Though you may remain physically tired here on earth, in Him, you have spiritual rest. Trust God with the faith of a little child, who can fall asleep in a carrier, with no worries from the past to haunt him, nor cares for the future to cause restlessness. Trust in Him to pick you up and carry you through all of life's struggles, both physical and spiritual.

> *Gracious Savior, gentle Shepherd,*
> *Children all are dear to Thee;*
> *Gathered with Thine arms, and carried*
> *In Thy bosom may we be;*
> *Sweetly, fondly, safely tended,*
> *From all want and danger free. (367:1)*

For Further Reading: Deuteronomy 1; Psalm 55

All-Consuming

"Take heed to yourselves, lest you forget the covenant of the Lord your God which He made with you....For the Lord your God is a consuming fire, a jealous God." Deuteronomy 4:23–24

God's jealousy as a raging fire? That's quite a picture to behold! When we reflect on our responsibilities as mothers, both to the physical and spiritual care of our children, God's wrathful inferno would leave any mother grief-stricken. As much as I try to live my faith in my actions each day, I fail. There are moments of laziness, moments when I lose my temper, moments of dissatisfaction.

But that same all-consuming fire of God's righteous anger at sin is appeased by His all-consuming compassion for sinners. That very love, that fervor, sent Jesus to the cross as our Sacrifice. "God made Him who had no sin to be sin for us, so that in Him we might become the righteousness of God" (2 Cor. 5:21).

Our sins deserve God's consuming fire, and our consciences know and feel our sin, but there is a remedy. We pray in our liturgy: "We poor sinners confess unto You that we are by nature sinful and unclean, and that we have sinned against you....We flee for refuge to Your infinite mercy, seeking and imploring Your grace, for the sake of our Lord Jesus Christ." In the person of Jesus, God's all-consuming fire is quenched by His all-consuming love, filling us up for lives of compassion to those in our midst.

> *If my sins give me alarm*
> *And my conscience grieve me,*
> *Let Thy cross my fear disarm;*
> *Peace of conscience give me.*
> *Grant that I may trust in Thee*
> *And Thy holy Passion;*
> *If His Son so loveth me,*
> *God must have compassion. (287:5)*

For Further Reading: Deuteronomy 4; 2 Corinthians 5

Blessings

"You shall therefore keep His statutes and His commandments which I command you today, that it may go well with you and with your children after you, and that you may prolong your days in the land which the Lord your God is giving you for all time." Deuteronomy 4:40

Do you have rules established in your family? What are they? Why did you establish them? I'll bet you made as many rules as possible, made them as difficult to follow as possible, and hope your children will fail so you can punish them severely. No? Of course not! The purpose of rules is to keep children safe and families running smoothly! We teach our children that when they follow our rules, they will be blessed.

The same goes with following God's laws. Deuteronomy is the last book of the Pentateuch, often collectively called the Book of the Law. Those who haven't read it thoroughly think it to be merely a list of rules. Certainly, there *are* many rules. But attached to those rules are numerous blessings. Who wouldn't want it to go well with them, and with their children after them? Who wouldn't want a prolonged life in the Promised Land? God gave His people a blueprint for success. When we remain under the umbrella of God's good commands, we also reap the spiritual benefits He promises. This is not because we have earned or deserved anything, but solely because of the redeeming death and resurrection of Jesus.

> *He lives to grant me rich supply;*
> *He lives to guide me with His eye.*
> *He lives to comfort me when faint;*
> *He lives to hear my soul's complaint.*
> *He lives to silence all my fears;*
> *He lives to wipe away my tears.*
> *He lives to calm my troubled heart;*
> *He lives all blessings to impart. (351:4,5)*

For Further Reading: Deuteronomy 4; John 1:17; Gal. 2:16

The "Perfect" House?

"You shall not covet your neighbor's wife; and you shall not desire your neighbor's house, his field, his male servant, his female servant, his ox, his donkey, or anything that is your neighbor's." Deuteronomy 5:21

Do you have a "perfect" house? I think most of us would admit ours is far from perfect. Whether it's a fixer-upper constantly needing attention, a city-dwelling you wish was in the country, a small place you wish was roomier, or a lack of home-decorating skills, we all struggle to find contentment in our abodes. Years ago, I decided to forgo perusing *Better Homes and Gardens* because of the angst and frustration it caused me regarding my own imperfect home, and the discontent and envy it caused me as I looked at what others possessed. Have you ever felt the same way?

Did you know God has the perfect house? I'm not talking about Heaven, though of course, that's perfect, too. I mean *you*, your heart! Yes, the Master Craftsman of the Universe makes His home in your heart. Having cleansed it in the waters of baptism, He scrubbed away the previously permanent stains of covetousness and envy of others' homes and lives. Our Heavenly Father has remodeled our hearts, stone upon stone, after the heart of Jesus. Not only does He deign to dwell in our hearts, but He makes us heirs to an even greater habitation—the mansions Christ prepares for us in Heaven while we journey through this life.

We are God's house of living stones,
Builded for His habitation;
He through baptismal grace us owns
Heirs of His wondrous salvation;
Were we but two His name to tell,
Yet He would deign with us to dwell,
With all His grace and His favor. (211:3)

For Further Reading: Deuteronomy 5; John 14:2–3

Look at Me!

"Therefore you shall be careful to do as the Lord your God has commanded you; you shall not turn aside to the right hand or to the left." Deuteronomy 5:32

"Look at me, Mom!" Every mom has heard these words, right? Like dozens of times during a single trip to the playground? We say them to our children, as well. I've been known to calmly, but sternly, take a child's face in my hands, peer into their eyes, and say, "Look at me!" When the child can't seem to focus on the matter at hand, attention vacillating from one thing to another, it becomes necessary for Mom to help the child reduce distraction and focus on the topic at hand.

God demands our undivided attention. He doesn't want us to run after the idols that the devil, the world, and our own sinful flesh hold before us. He tells us in the verse above, "No more distractions!" But thankfully, it's not so much about us looking to God, and keeping our eyes on Him. If it were, we'd have lost our way years ago! Even while our feet are straying from the clearly marked path, God's got His eyes on us, guiding us and protecting us. In the Lord's Supper, He removes all distractions, placing forgiveness into our mouths. He takes our proverbial faces in His hands, saying, "Look at Me, for the forgiveness of your sins."

A pledge of peace from God I see
When Thy pure eyes are turned to me
To show me Thy good pleasure.
Jesus, Thy Spirit and Thy Word,
Thy body and Thy blood, afford
My soul its dearest treasure.
Keep me Kindly
In Thy favor,
O my Savior!
Thou wilt cheer me;
Thy Word calls me to draw near Thee. (167:4)

For Further Reading: Deuteronomy 5; Hebrews 12

When My Strength Cannot Avail Me

"Hear, O Israel: The Lord our God, the Lord is one! You shall love the Lord your God with all your heart, with all your soul, and with all your strength. Deuteronomy 6:4–5

God demands that I love Him with all of my heart. And with all of my soul. But with all of my strength? Well, that almost seems like an insult to God! With all the needs and demands of motherhood, sometimes I don't have much strength left. Some days, it's hard to get out of bed, much less love the Lord my God with all of my strength!

If you feel the same way, you are in good company. Biblical company, in fact. Samson, a man previously known for his strength, prayed for God's strength to punish his enemies (Jdg. 16). Nehemiah asked for the Lord to strengthen his hands to rebuild Jerusalem's wall. Isaiah found his strength and his song in God. Even the patriarch Abraham was strengthened in faith (Rom. 4:20). All of these diverse historical figures had one thing in common: They didn't muster up strength from inside themselves. Rather, they looked to the One True God to supply their strength, day by day.

God's Son began His life weak and helpless, laid in a feeding trough. He began His ministry weak and tempted, vulnerable in the desert. In a weakened state from the scourging, Jesus died on the cross, making you right with God, filling you with His strength. And when God supplies your strength, you are strong, indeed.

All that for my soul is needful He with loving care provides,
Nor of that is He unheedful Which my body needs besides.
When my strength cannot avail me,
When my pow'rs can do no more,
Doth my God His strength outpour; In my need He doth not fail me.
All things else have but their day,
God's great love abides for aye. (448:3)

For Further Reading: Deuteronomy 6; Psalm 68:35

Matins

"You shall teach them diligently to your children, and shall talk of them when you sit in your house, when you walk by the way, when you lie down, and when you rise up." Deuteronomy 6:7

Rising up is, admittedly, not my strong point. I usually stay in bed until the last possible moment. I'm definitely not a morning person. Talking about God's commands and teaching them diligently to my children (in the morning, when I rise up) is not something I am capable of doing on my own. If I retain my composure at all, I call it success.

What about you? Are you a morning person? What do you do if you're not? Or what about other times in your day when you find your lips glued shut, without the spiritual encouragement for your children that you ought to have? An order of worship called Matins, traditionally prayed at the break of day, gives us utterance from the Psalms: "O Lord, open my lips. And my mouth shall show forth Your praise." And what about when you're just plain too pooped to stop that nagging from oozing off your tongue? Instead: "Make haste, O God, to deliver me. Make haste to help me, O Lord." And what about when you find yourself muttering about yet more jobs to do and people to care for and demands to be met? "Glory be to the Father and to the Son and to the Holy Ghost. As it was in the beginning, is now, and ever shall be: forevermore. Amen. Alleluia!" Christ's redeeming love, bestowed upon us by the Holy Spirit, opens our lips, delivers us from our sins, and empowers us to give glory to the Trinity.

Say it, pray it, chant it in the morning when you rise up, or whenever your own words fail you. Thank God for putting the words of Scripture, found in Matins, on our tongues all day long.

> *Take my life and let it be*
> *Consecrated, Lord, to Thee.*
> *Take my moments and my days;*
> *Let them flow in ceaseless praise. (444:1)*

For Further Reading: Deuteronomy 6; Psalms 51 and 70

Increase

"He will also bless the fruit of your womb and the fruit of your land, your grain and your new wine and your oil, the increase of your cattle and the offspring of your flock, in the land of which He swore to your fathers to give you. You shall be blessed above all peoples; there shall not be a male or female barren among you or among your livestock." Deuteronomy 7:13–14

If you were to receive a reward for a mothering job well done, what would you want? Someone to cook a meal for you? Cash? A gift certificate for a massage and haircut? How about jewelry? Our cultural expectations of rewards and blessings are very different than God's. God's reward is new life. And He gives it without any merit or worthiness in us, all as a gift. He gives and increases, and then He gives some more!

With God's blessing comes responsibility. Do you find yourself weighed down with numerous responsibilities? If you do, consider yourself favored by God! Your unique calling as your husband's wife and your children's mother are your most fundamental and irreplaceable vocations here on earth. God has made you His own in baptism and He will give you the help you need for the increased responsibilities you have throughout life. And even when we turn from Him in sin and irresponsibility, His grace increases all the more (Rom. 5:20). He is always available for us, His unending reservoir of forgiveness overflowing when we repent.

Hear us, dear Father, when we pray
For needed help from day to day
That as Thy children we may live,
Whom Thou in Baptism didst receive.
Lord, when we fall and sin doth stain,
Absolve and lift us up again;
And through the Sacrament increase
Our faith till we depart in peace. (551:3,4)

For Further Reading: Deuteronomy 7 and 28; Luke 12:48

Full Bellies

*"When you have eaten and are full, then you shall bless the Lord
your God for the good land which He has given you."*
Deuteronomy 8:10

In my Lutheran culture growing up, we said the "common table prayer" and "returned thanks" before partaking of a meal. I still think this is a wonderful practice, but a bit different from what the Lord instructs above. He says to eat, be filled, *and then* praise Him for His gifts.

I don't think the point of the passage is specifically to instruct believers when to pray about their food, though. It's just another divine reminder that all our blessings, including the Fourth Petition gift of daily bread, come from God. So, while you're in your daily routine of menu-planning, thawing frozen meat, chopping produce to be used later, washing those dishes with caked-on food, and wiping up the table after mealtime, recall with delight the blessings of food God has bestowed on your family.

What amazing abundance we have, even when our budgets are tight! What variety and creativity God used in making a diversity of foods for us to enjoy! What blessing that God's gift of science is making clear the most healthful types of foods for us to enjoy and feed to our families! It is a privilege, though often more work than we would like, that God uses us as mothers to be a channel of His gift of food to our husbands and children. God is good and has blessed us abundantly—whether your supper tonight is a four-course scratch gourmet meal from Whole Foods, or from a cereal box!

> *Great God, we praise Thy gracious care,*
> *Which does our daily bread prepare;*
> *O bless the earthly food we take,*
> *And feed our souls for Jesus' sake. (600:1)*

For Further Reading: Deuteronomy 8; Psalm 145:15–16

Eating Your Children

"You shall eat the fruit of your own body, the flesh of your sons
and your daughters whom the Lord your God has given you,
in the siege and desperate straits in which your enemy
shall distress you." Deuteronomy 28:53

Perhaps the title and the Scripture verse above gave you pause. Hold on to your stomachs for a minute while you read. This is not a devotion for the faint of gut. Here and in several other Bible passages (Jer. 19:9; Lam. 4:10; Ez. 5:10), the Lord prophesies that if people curse Him, their own lives would become so cursed that parents would consume their children.

When choosing Scriptures for these devotions, I really, really wanted to skip this verse. This is my biggest nightmare. I shake in my boots when I imagine whether the evil in our world could ever be so great that Satan could tempt me to consider murdering and eating my own precious children. How could this passage possibly encourage and uplift a mother?

Well, take heart, for you yourself are God's beloved, His own. He has already given the flesh of His Son so that this curse will not fall upon you! He strengthens you with Jesus' body and blood to combat temptation. No matter what horror may come in this world, no matter if your sin is so unimaginably treacherous: remember God's covenant. Satan cannot place a charge against God's elect, for Jesus has already washed your sins away. You are safe from accusations in Christ's hands. Nothing, no abhorrent sin, no shockingly gruesome future world, can separate us from God.

> *His oath, His covenant, and blood*
> *Support me in the whelming flood;*
> *When ev'ry earthly prop gives way,*
> *He then is all my Hope and Stay.*
> *On Christ, the solid Rock, I stand;*
> *All other ground is sinking sand. (197:3)*

For Further Reading: Deuteronomy 28; Romans 8

A Profound Choice

"I have set before you today life and good, death and evil,... blessing and cursing; therefore choose life, that both you and your descendants may live." Deuteronomy 30:15,19

Every day we are forced to make choices. If your mornings are anything like mine, that first choice is forced too early, with the question of "Mom, what's for breakfast?" In the passage above, God puts before the Israelites a very important choice. Will they worship the Lord their God and Him only, choosing life? Or will they follow the gods of this world, choosing death?

We are already part of God's family through baptism, but we daily have the same choice set before us as the Israelites. We can trust God and His promises (life), even when that path seems difficult, and order our actions according to that trust. Or we can question and doubt God's goodness, choosing our attitude based on idolizing our own thoughts and desires (death).

Each and every day, each and every moment, this profound choice is before you. Simply by living your calling as a sanctified Christian to serve your family, you live clinging to life. With God's help, you daily drown the old Adam in you as you remember your baptism, and bring forth the new (wo)man who lives before God in righteousness and purity. Though your day is filled with so many choices, be at peace knowing that every act fulfilling your vocation is a profound choice, living amidst the promises of God given to you in Christ.

> *I know no life divided,*
> *O Lord of life, from Thee;*
> *In Thee is life provided*
> *For all mankind and me;*
> *I know no death, O Jesus,*
> *Because I live in Thee;*
> *Thy death it is which frees us*
> *From death eternally. (531:2)*

For Further Reading: Deuteronomy 30; Proverbs 3:5-6

Sanctifying Fear

"Be strong and of good courage, do not fear nor be afraid of them; for the Lord your God, He is the One who goes with you.... He will be with you, He will not leave you nor forsake you; do not fear nor be dismayed." Deuteronomy 31:6,8

We don't face the towering nations of Canaan like Joshua did. But, I have been known to cower in the bedroom for a few minutes, fearful of the little people I will find when I come out! We often have big fears: How can I continue to stay at home/afford daycare with the finances as they are? Will this child's illness ever improve? Am I slowly going insane from all the pressures of mothering? God knows our little fears, too: Will the leftovers stretch to feed us all at lunch? When will I ever get time alone with my husband again? Will I literally explode if the toddler asks "why" one more time?

Every day, we fight our fears, working to trust God. Every day, God is faithful and He fights the source of our fears, giving us reason for courage. The separation from Him that we deserve was suffered on the cross by Christ, Who was forsaken because of our sins. We no longer have to fear His absence. God doesn't promise to safeguard us from life's problems, but He does promise to be with us every step of the way, through all of our fears, little or big.

Not only does God uphold us during fearful times, He also brings about good through our troubles. How is God working in this situation to strengthen your faith or develop Godly virtue in your character? When you are fearful, cast your anxiety on the Lord, looking for blessings in your struggles.

> *"Fear not, I am with you; O be not dismayed,*
> *For I am your God and will still give you aid;*
> *I'll strengthen you, help you, and cause you to stand,*
> *Upheld by My righteous, omnipotent hand.*
> *When through the deep waters I call you to go,*
> *The rivers of sorrow shall not overflow,*
> *For I will be with you in trouble to bless*
> *And sanctify to you your deepest distress." (521:2,3)*

For Further Reading: Deuteronomy 31; Isaiah 43:1-21

Canticles for Christ

"'Write down this song for yourselves, and teach it to the children of Israel; put it in their mouths, that this song may be a witness for Me against the children of Israel.'...Moses therefore wrote this song the same day, and taught it to the children of Israel." Deuteronomy 31:19,22

When we think of music and songs coming from the Bible, we often think of the Psalms, similar to Biblical poetry. But right here toward the end of the Pentateuch, we find a song which God himself composed. (See Deut. 32:1–43 to read the song in its entirety.) The church has given the name *canticle* to any Scriptural song which comes from a place other than the Psalms, including this song of Moses.

Although this song is largely a song of prediction of future condemnation, I find it fascinating that God used the medium of music and singing to teach the Israelites through Moses one last time before he died on Mt. Nebo. Music is a divine vehicle through which God's people commit His words and wisdom to heart. Such a treasury lays at our fingertips and lips when we study our hymnals and the rich renditions of Gospel-centered Scriptures found therein. Children often find it easier to memorize lines of rhyming poetry, rather than long lines of Scriptural prose, both of which contain the same Biblical truths. There are even some musical settings for hymns or Luther's Small Catechism on CD for those of us who cannot play along on a piano or sing very well. May we always make use of God's gift of music, both to remind us of His love in Christ and also to praise Him in our homes every day!

Be this, while life is mine, my canticle divine:
"May Jesus Christ be praised!"
Be this th'eternal song through all the ages long:
"May Jesus Christ be praised!" (85:6)

For Further Reading: Deuteronomy 31; Isaiah 12:2

A Quiet Chamber

"Now see that I, even I, am He, And there is no God besides Me; I kill and I make alive; I wound and I heal; Nor is there any who can deliver from My hand." Deuteronomy 32:39

Our culture bombards women with the message that timing is everything when it comes to starting a family. Wait until your education is through, your finances certain, and your dreams achieved. But as Christians, we know that God calls children blessings regardless of the circumstances regarding their conception and birth. God is the source of life, and He doesn't make mistakes.

Whether you have experienced the heartbreak of infertility, the devastation of miscarriage or stillbirth, or the blessing of many children with the burden of fear for the future: trust in the Lord. Whether your family is smaller than you have prayed for, larger than you had anticipated, or somewhere between, know that our Heavenly Father, the Maker, Redeemer, and Comforter, is in control of that quiet chamber called the womb. The devil may fight, the world may whisper, and our own sinful flesh may despair, but God kills and makes alive. He's got the whole world, and our little bitty babies, in His hands.

God placed the Promised Child into the womb of the Virgin Mary 2,000 years ago. It didn't fit the cultural expectations of the time, nor did it fit in with the expectations of His own people who were watching and waiting for the promised Messiah. But the Babe in Mary's womb lived and died to redeem all others who have come from the womb—you, me, your children and mine, our parents and grandparents, and generations yet unborn. No life or death is granted without God's providence and control, with eternity in His long-term plans. May Jesus, the Holy Child, quiet your heart as you wait on His timing and purposes for your womb.

Ah, dearest Jesus, holy Child,
Make Thee a bed, soft, undefiled,
Within my heart, that it may be
A quiet chamber kept for Thee. (124:13)

For Further Reading: Deuteronomy 32; Luke 2

Baptismal Reminders

"When your children ask in time to come, saying, 'What do these stones mean to you?' Then you shall answer them that the waters of the Jordan were cut off before the ark of the covenant of the Lord; when it crossed over the Jordan, the waters of the Jordan were cut off. And these stones shall be for a memorial to the children of Israel forever." Joshua 4:6–7

In the passage above, the Israelites had just crossed the Jordan river, embarking on the last leg of their 40-year journey in the desert after the Exodus from Egypt. They were instructed by their leaders to set up a new tradition, a tradition not unlike the Passover, where a conversation between parents and children glorified God and ensured that His Word would be passed down the generations. In this case, one leader from each tribe was to place a stone which came from the Jordan River onto a pile in the city of Gilgal. It was a visual reminder of God's grace in safely passing through the waters of the Jordan, and a conversation starter for all of the future generations, curious about the purpose of that big pile of rocks!

Family traditions are well and good and bring us together around a common identity. But faith-based traditions are even better. Just as the Israelites passed through both the waters of the Red Sea and the waters of the Jordan on dry land, God has saved you and your children through the washing waters of your baptism. Perhaps a shell, candle, or baptismal certificate can spark conversation about this Heavenly gift. With God's help, daily remember this blessed gift and the peace it brings to your family.

Once in the blest baptismal waters
I put on Christ and made Him mine;
Now numbered with God's sons and daughters,
I share His peace and love divine. My God, for Jesus' sake I pray
Thy peace may bless my dying day. (483:8)

For Further Reading: Joshua 4; Romans 6:3–5

The All-Inclusive Curriculum

"There was not a word of all that Moses had commanded which
Joshua did not read before all the assembly of Israel,
with the women, the little ones, and the strangers
who were living among them." Joshua 8:35

In my early days of parenting, I wanted to have just the right curriculum for teaching the Bible to my children: challenging to my older kids, but not too lofty that the younger ones would be lost. I scoured various devotion and Bible story books. There are many good ones out there! But, I could never shake the feeling that someone was always left out. I wanted the perfect "all-inclusive" curriculum. God put many wiser Christians in my path, however, who reminded me that God's Word itself is at everyone's level, as in the account above. We don't have to find some curriculum or program outside of God's Word, because His Word itself can penetrate everyone's soul, big or little, advanced or simple. Reading the Bible aloud is accessible to every listener.

In the First Petition to the Lord's Prayer, Luther teaches us that finding the "perfect" Bible story book isn't what hallows God's name. "God's name is hallowed when His Word is taught in its truth and purity, and we as the children of God live holy lives according to it. This grant us, dear Father in Heaven!" You and your children, no matter your age or level of theological grasp, are part of God's family. Schooled through His Word and Sacraments to receive forgiveness in Christ, He gives us the all-inclusive package deal!

> *But still Thy Law and Gospel, Lord,*
> *Have lessons more divine;*
> *Not earth stands firmer than Thy Word,*
> *Nor stars so nobly shine.*
> *Thy Word is everlasting truth; How pure is ev'ry page!*
> *That holy Book shall guide our youth*
> *And well support our age. (176:4,5)*

For Further Reading: Joshua 8; Hebrews 4:12

Ask God's Counsel

"[The men of Israel] did not ask counsel of the Lord. So Joshua made peace with [the Gibeonites], and made a covenant with them to let them live....And it happened at the end of three days ...that [the Israelites] heard that [the Gibeonites] were their neighbors who dwelt near them." Joshua 9:14–16

Those sneaky Gibeonites, masquerading as foreigners and begging Israel for mercy and a covenant of peace! The Israelites had formerly been instructed to destroy the peoples living in the land of Canaan and take over the land with God's blessing. That first sentence in the passage above clearly points out their mistake: they didn't pray about their decision, and that hasty decision led to much suffering.

As mothers, we make hundreds of decisions a day, many on behalf of our dear children. God invites us to pray about these choices that weigh on our hearts: What kind of education should we pursue? How should we discipline? Even seemingly trivial things like which car seat to purchase! He is our true Father and we are His true children, so we can ask Him anything with all boldness and confidence. Jesus assured His disciples of God's loving care before He sent them out to preach: even the very hairs on their heads were numbered! He grants you that same individual attention and care. Come to Him in prayer with all of your parenting troubles and decisions!

> *God is my Comfort and my Trust,*
> *My Hope and Life abiding;*
> *And to His counsel wise and just,*
> *I yield, in Him confiding.*
> *The very hairs,*
> *His Word declares,*
> *Upon my head He numbers.*
> *By night and day*
> *God is my Stay,*
> *He never sleeps nor slumbers. (477:2)*

For Further Reading: Joshua 9; Matthew 10:30

Divine Intervention

"Then Joshua spoke to the Lord in the day when the Lord delivered up the Amorites before the children of Israel, and he said in the sight of Israel: 'Sun, stand still over Gibeon; And Moon, in the Valley of Aijalon.' So the sun stood still, And the moon stopped, Till the people had revenge Upon their enemies." Joshua 10:12–13

Imagine the sun standing still! It must have been an amazing sight—God lengthening the day to ensure the battle would be won by His people. Nothing is impossible for God. He's the only One we need on our side, fighting for us.

Sometimes frustrations in our own lives seem irritatingly impossible—whether they are behavior problems with a child, marital strife, or feeling up against a brick wall battling with our own sense of purpose. The struggles are real!

While these issues are all important to God because we are important to Him, He is in no way limited by them. Just as He performed miracles with the created orbs in the atmosphere for His children in the desert, He can perform miracles in your life, too. In fact, whenever we read God's Word and are nourished by His body and blood, we witness God's miraculous forgiveness in our hearts. We have no need to be clever enough to solve our own problems, when we've got the God of the Universe, the Worker of Miracles, fighting our battles for us!

Help me henceforth, O God of grace,
Help me on each occasion,
Help me in each and ev'ry place,
Help me through Jesus' Passion.
Help me in life and death, O God,
Help me through Jesus' dying blood;
Help me as Thou hast helped me. (71:3)

For Further Reading: Joshua 10; Luke 1:37

Promises Fulfilled

*"Not one of all the Lord's good promises to Israel failed;
every one was fulfilled." Joshua 21:45 (NIV)*

The Israelites had escaped slavery, sojourned in the
wilderness, and defeated their enemies, all with the Lord's help.
They had overcome. Now, each tribe had been assigned its
homeland in the territory promised long ago to their ancestor,
Abraham.

God had sworn that He would fulfill His Word. Who but God
can keep such a promise? Certainly no human. No Israelite. No
mother. We've gone back on promises. Even those promises we
really intend to keep can be thwarted by powers outside of our
control. But God Almighty, the Ruler of Heaven and Earth keeps
His promises. However, He does so in His own time and in His
own way.

The Israelites waited centuries for God to bring about their
redemption. And centuries later, God fulfilled His ultimate
promise of redeeming humankind with an ironic twist—the birth,
death, and resurrection of God Himself in the man Jesus. Despite
any promises you have broken in your life, every promise of God
is yea and amen in Christ.

Though we often cannot see God's plan clearly in our lives,
once we join Him in the Heavenly mansions, we will be able to say
with all confidence, "Not one of all the Lord's good promises to
me failed; every one was fulfilled."

> *God's Word a treasure is to me,*
> *Through sorrow's night my sun shall be,*
> *The shield of faith in battle.*
> *The Father's hand hath written there*
> *My title as His child and heir,*
> *"The kingdom's thine forever."*
> *That promise faileth never. (586:2)*

For Further Reading: Joshua 21 and 23:14; 2 Corinthians 1:20

Claimed

"When all that generation had been gathered to their fathers,
another generation arose after them who did not know the Lord
nor the work which He had done for Israel." Judges 2:10

This is a great fear for mothers, isn't it? Once our children have left our homes (or even while they are still here!), might they fall away from faith and forsake the Lord our Savior? What a huge responsibility we have to pass on God's Word to our children and children's children!

We should rightly feel the weight of this duty. However, we also rest in the Lord's hands as we perform this work. We remember the Spirit, His Spirit, given to our children in the sacrament of baptism. That water applied to a child's head in baptism is "a gracious water of life and washing of regeneration in the Holy Spirit, as St. Paul says, Titus 3:5–8: 'According to His mercy He saved us, by the washing of regeneration and renewing of the Holy Spirit, whom He poured out on us abundantly through Jesus Christ our Savior; that having been justified by His grace, we should become heirs according to the hope of eternal life. This is a faithful saying.'"

Though we train our children and pray for them, their faith is ultimately in God's good hands. He has put His name onto each of us, and onto our children, at our baptisms. He has claimed our souls. We immerse ourselves in this comfort, even when we or our children go astray.

O bless Thy Word to all the young;
Let them, Thy truth possessing,
Bear witness true with heart and tongue,
Their faith and ours confessing.
From mother's arms Thy grace
With love did them embrace;
Baptized into Thy name, As Thine Thou didst them claim.
O Lord, as Thine now own them! (514:2)

For Further Reading: Judges 2; Titus 3

Patience, Patience

"Gideon replied, 'If the Lord is with us, why has all this happened to us? Where are all his wonders that our ancestors told us about when they said, "Did not the Lord bring us up out of Egypt?" But now the Lord has abandoned us and given us into the hand of Midian."' Judges 6:13 (NIV)

The Israelites had been free from the Egyptians for many years. And in their freedom, they forgot Jehovah and their covenant with Him. They turned from God's ways; they did evil in God's sight. So the Lord chastised His people with the scourge of the Midianites who consistently destroyed the crops of the Israelites right before harvest, leaving man and animal hungry. It looked to Gideon as if all hope was gone. But God had not forgotten His covenant with His dear children.

When Gideon speaks the words above, an angel had just appeared, calling him to deliver God's people out of the oppression of Midian. The very man whom God was to use to end the difficulties of His people, doubted that a mighty God would do just that. What patience God had with Gideon! And what patience He has with us!

God not only puts up with the weak faith of His people, He heals us of our unbelief! He truly knows human frailty: Jesus became a man as part of His humiliation in order to redeem us from it! When we doubt God's promises or are impatient with those in our care, God covers our iniquities with the blood of Christ.

> *Show me now a Father's love*
> *And His tender patience.*
> *Heal my wounded soul; remove*
> *These too sore temptations.*
> *I am weak; Father, speak*
> *Thou of peace and gladness;*
> *Comfort Thou my sadness. (454:2)*

For Further Reading: Judges 6; Romans 15:5–6

God's Purpose Overcomes Weakness

"Samson said to his father, 'Get [a Philistine wife] for me, for she pleases me well.' But his father and mother did not know that it was of the Lord—that He was seeking an occasion to move against the Philistines." Judges 14:3–4

Whenever I read this part of the story of Samson in Bible History, I want to shout, "No, Samson! No! You—a judge over Israel and a Nazirite set apart—should know better! You need to seek a God-fearing wife!" That's probably what Samson's mother and father were thinking, too.

I suppose the same is true of God as He looks down on us living our lives and making choices. "No, my child! You should know better than that!" We sin with our thoughts, words, and deeds. We sin by acts of both commission and omission. We are steeped in a sinful nature from birth (Psalm 51:5). But God does not leave us wallowing in sin. Graciously, our Heavenly Father has given us the tools of confession and absolution, as described in the Catechism: "Confession consists of two parts: one, that we confess our sins; the other, that we receive absolution, or forgiveness, from the pastor or confessor as from God himself, and in no way doubt, but firmly believe that our sins are thereby forgiven before God in heaven." Thankfully, not only does the Lord wash away our sins, He even uses our sinful weaknesses to accomplish His purposes, just like He did in the life of Samson.

> *What shall I, frail man, be pleading,*
> *Who for me be interceding*
> *When the just are mercy needing?*
> *King of Majesty tremendous,*
> *Who dost free salvation send us,*
> *Fount of pity, then befriend us!*
> *Righteous Judge, for sin's pollution*
> *Grant Thy gift of absolution*
> *Ere the Day of Retribution. (537:3)*

For Further Reading: Judges 14; Romans 8:28

Held Together

"Entreat me not to leave you, Or to turn back from following after you; For wherever you go, I will go; And wherever you lodge, I will lodge; Your people shall be my people, And your God, my God." Ruth 1:16

Aside from the fact that I responded with this verse when my husband asked me to marry him, this is one of my favorite Bible passages. (My husband likes to tease me that I never did say "yes" to him!) The text is so poetic; it also shows the beauty of commitment to one another that is needed to have a solid foundation in a family. We trust that we will be there for one another.

Even though we'd like to think we can make and keep Ruth's promise to those we love, often, we still fail them. How many times haven't you disappointed a child? Our own commitments waver and fail. But when God's unwavering love toward us is the foundation upon which our family is built, we are inspired. We recall how our Savior gave His life to cover our failures. He names us His own precious children in the waters of baptism. We remember that the Holy Spirit lives in our hearts and empowers us to put away our selfishness and truly love those in our care, regardless of the cost. Sometimes, like Ruth, this means giving up the life we knew and the comfort of familiarity in order to follow God's ways. But we trust that He bolsters each and every step we take, confident that Christ holds our family together.

Christ is made the sure foundation,
Christ, the head and cornerstone,
Chosen of the Lord, and precious,
Binding all the Church in one,
Holy Zion's help for ever,
And her confidence alone. (8:1)

For Further Reading: Ruth 1; 1 Corinthians 3:9–16

Lent to Live

"For this child I prayed, and the Lord has granted me my petition which I asked of Him. Therefore I also have lent him to the Lord; as long as he lives he shall be lent to the Lord."
1 Samuel 1:27–28

Hannah's heartfelt prayer of thanksgiving for her son Samuel has been echoed by many a Christian mother over the centuries. In verse 5 of this chapter, Scripture tells us that the Lord had closed Hannah's womb up to this point. We don't know God's reason for this, but we do know He heard Hannah, and cared for her, just as He does for us. Not only did God grant Hannah her request, He blessed her abundantly beyond all she could ever have hoped for, blessing her with five additional children (2:21)! All of our needs and wants, cares and concerns, are known to Him, including our concerns about fertility—whether we yearn for a child, like Hannah, or are fearful of yet another pregnancy.

Some of us are thrilled by the new life within our wombs; others are tempted to worry about how to care for a new child (and also ourselves). But whatever the context of our bearing new life, we acknowledge that it is the Lord who plans each new life and gives each new child. He has a marvelous plan for each and every one of us.

As Hannah loaned her little son Samuel to the Lord for His work, so also, with God's help, we raise our children to His service. We loan our own bodies to the Lord to bear and nurture the lives He sends us, just like Hannah. And we rest in the blessing of God's Word and baptism to keep our children in the faith so they may live their lives in God's service, just like Samuel.

Since by this water and the Word
We're born again, we thank You, Lord.
Through life and death Yours may we be,
Your children through eternity. (248:6)

For Further Reading: 1 Samuel 1; Ephesians 2:10

Parental Responsibility

"For I have told him that I will judge his house forever for the iniquity which he knows, because his sons made themselves vile, and he did not restrain them." 1 Samuel 3:13

In this prophecy, God informs Samuel of the judgment He will carry out on the family of Eli. Eli's sons served in the house of the Lord, but had corrupted the practices God had set forth. They were an example of wickedness to the people of Israel. In this chapter of Scripture, God demonstrates to all parents, in no uncertain terms, that the failure to restrain sin in one's children is a sin in itself.

It is a large part of the office of parenthood to monitor the behavior of our children and check it, discipling them as they learn to recognize sin, repent of it, and grow in Christ-like behavior by the power of the Holy Spirit. How often have you shirked this responsibility for other less significant aspects of parenthood? But, no matter how hard you might try to get your priorities straight, you will still never be a perfect mother.

God was the perfect Father for His Son, Jesus. Although Jesus led a perfect life, His Father was compelled to punish Him on your behalf, for all your imperfections, including those times when you have not checked your own sin, or the sins of your children. Resting in the knowledge that God was the perfect parent in your place and that Jesus was judged on the cross for both your sins and the sins of your children, rejoice! Trust in the Lord and pray that He will guide you in discipling your children for His glory.

> *O gently call those gone astray*
> *That they may find the saving way!*
> *Let ev'ry conscience sore oppressed*
> *In Thee find peace and heav'nly rest. (198:3)*

For Further Reading: 1 Samuel 3; Hebrews 12:11

The Queen of Vocations

"And Saul answered and said, 'Am I not a Benjamite, of the smallest of the tribes of Israel, and my family the least of all the families of the tribe of Benjamin? Why then do you speak like this to me?'" 1 Samuel 9:21

Eli and his sons had died, and now Samuel was the prophet of the Lord in Israel. Samuel was well-loved by the people, but he was getting old. Samuel's sons did not walk in God's ways; and so, the people demanded a king be placed over them, rather than have Samuel's ungodly sons rule them. God chose Saul as that king.

In the words of the text, Saul is replying to Samuel, who has invited him to come and eat with his company. Samuel has already been told by the Lord that Saul will be king. Saul acknowledges his humble background. Often, humble circumstances are exactly what God desires in His servants, to bring Himself great glory.

Worldly vanity looks upon the vocation of motherhood as frivolous, demanding that women must prove themselves with education or a career. True, motherhood may appear to be the most humble of jobs to the world; but it is truly the queen of all earthly vocations. Our very Savior came from humble circumstances to serve and save us sinners. Forgive us, Father, for the times we grumble at this beautiful and exalted work you have given us to do!

> *The world seeks to be praised*
> *And honored by the mighty,*
> *Yet never once reflects*
> *That they are frail and flighty.*
> *But what I truly prize*
> *Above all things is He,*
> *My Jesus, He alone.*
> *What is the world to me! (446:3)*

For Further Reading: 1 Samuel 9; John 13:1-17

Repentant Hearts He'll Not Despise

"Then Samuel said to the people, 'Do not fear. You have done all this wickedness; yet do not turn aside from following the Lord, but serve the Lord with all your heart.'" 1 Samuel 12:20

Some coronation speech, huh? The Israelites had asked for a king. God had given them one, but Samuel told it how it was: It was their own wickedness which caused them to trust an earthly king, rather than the Heavenly King who had brought them out of Egypt! In addition to Samuel's message, Jehovah sent frightening thunder and rain out of season, which left the Israelites quaking in their sandals, begging for their lives!

How much like the Israelites are we! We think our own plans will bring about the best outcome, rather than waiting on the Lord. We trust in parenting magazines that tell us we'll be fine if we just "follow our hearts," blatantly denying that we struggle with sin in our hearts, all the while being God's saints. We find time for all sorts of diversions in our lives, putting aside the efficacious Word of God. Lord, have mercy!

God records Samuel's words to the Israelites; they are a powerful accusation for us as well! We ourselves have heaped wickedness upon wickedness, yet the Lord still desires that we turn from our evil ways and follow Him. "The old Adam in us should, by daily contrition and repentance, be drowned and die with all sins and evil lusts; and that a new man daily come forth and arise, who shall live before God in righteousness and purity forever." Serve the Lord with all your heart! He's the only King whose compassion is merciful and abundant, even giving His own life as a ransom for yours.

> *O Zion's Daughter, rise*
> *To meet thy lowly King;*
> *Repentant hearts He'll not despise,*
> *Forgiveness He doth bring. (99:3)*

For Further Reading: 1 Samuel 12; Psalm 103:8

"What?!"

"Saul said to [Samuel], 'Blessed are you of the Lord! I have performed the commandment of the Lord.' But Samuel said, 'What then is this bleating of the sheep in my ears, and the lowing of the oxen which I hear?'" 1 Samuel 15:13–14

"Have you cleaned your room?" "Sure, Mom!" "Then, what's this stuff all over your floor?" "Have you finished your homework?" "You bet, Mom!" "Then, why are you having a difficult time reciting your memory work?" "How's it going watching your baby sister?" "Fine, Mom!" "Then, why do I hear her screaming in the other room?"

Our kids always want to answer us in the affirmative, but when we examine their actions, sometimes the task falls far short of our expectations. So goes the situation with Saul and Samuel. Saul was sent by God to utterly destroy the Amalekites, leaving nothing alive. He claims he executed God's judgment, as he had been directed, but the prophet's ears tell him otherwise. Saul had spared the life of King Agag, as well as many good-looking animals, fearing his own people above the Lord (verse 24).

As mothers, we are able to forgive our children for their sins of disobedience and excuses because we ourselves have behaved in the same manner toward our Heavenly Father, and He has fully and freely forgiven us! We know our rebellion against God breaks the First Commandment, but instead of punishment, the richness of God's mercy reigns. Rather than take the kingdom from us, as He did from Saul, God gives us the kingdom of His Son! What a precious paradox!

> *By grace! O mark this word of promise*
> *When thou art by thy sins oppressed,*
> *When Satan plagues thy troubled conscience,*
> *And when thy heart is seeking rest.*
> *What reason cannot comprehend*
> *God by His grace to thee doth send. (226:3)*

For Further Reading: 1 Samuel 15; Hebrews 12:28

The Battle is the Lord's

"Then David said to the Philistine, 'You come to me with a sword, with a spear, and with a javelin. But I come to you in the name of the Lord of hosts, the God of the armies of Israel, whom you have defied. This day the Lord will deliver you into my hand.... Then all this assembly shall know that the Lord does not save with sword and spear; for the battle is the Lord's, and He will give you into our hands.'" 1 Samuel 17:45–47

This Bible story is one of the most famous in the Old Testament. But it's so much more than the underdog we all want to win going up against a giant. It is one small episode in the epic war between good and evil, where both in this story and in the end, God triumphs. Through this passage, we're reminded that in all stories, God is the winner.

Whether your battles are with toddlers, teens, or somewhere in between, the battle is the Lord's. Whether your battles are with your own failures, attitudes, and addictions, or someone else's, the battle is the Lord's.

What are you battling? Who are you battling? These are important, introspective questions, but they put the emphasis in the wrong place...on you and your power! Instead, you already know the answers to these questions: Who's battling? And Who is battling for you? No matter what battles we're fighting, we already know how the story ends! We're the redeemed and victorious recipients of the greatest victory in all the universe's tales: Jesus' death and resurrection.

Fighting, we shall be victorious
By the blood of Christ our Lord;
On our foreheads, bright and glorious,
Shines the witness of His Word;
Spear and shield on battlefield,
His great name; we cannot yield. (217:3)

For Further Reading: 1 Samuel 17; Deuteronomy 20:1

Our Balm in Sorrow

"Then David and the people who were with him lifted up their
voices and wept, until they had no more power to weep."
1 Samuel 30:4

The city of Ziklag had just been sacked and burned to the ground by the enemies of David and his men. This was pretty significant, as all of their families had been living there. The women and children had been spared, but kidnapped and carried off into the wilderness.

David had a considerable reason to cry. He can also be found weeping in several other Scripture passages. When his son Absalom took over his capital city, David hiked up the Mount of Olives, weeping with all of his people (2 Sam. 15:30). After his servant announced the death of his son, David cried out again and again, wishing he could trade his life for that of his son (2 Sam. 18:33).

In two separate passages of Scripture, David is called a man after God's own heart (1 Sam. 13:13–14; Acts 13:22), and yet, he cried when tragedy struck his life. To cry out to the Lord is not necessarily a sign of weak faith—Jesus wept at the tomb of His dear friend Lazarus. We cannot avoid physical and emotional pain while we dwell in this sinful world. But even amidst our most difficult circumstances, remember Who is with you. Christ Himself experienced pain as a man here on earth. He is no stranger to your trials, and He hurts with you. He has a plan to bring an end to your suffering, rescuing you just as He did David. Through His death and resurrection, Heaven is yours for all eternity, even while you strive in this world.

Grant us Thy peace throughout our earthly life,
Our Balm in sorrow and our Stay in strife.
Then, when Thy voice shall bid our conflict cease,
Call us, O Lord, to Thine eternal peace. (597:4)

For Further Reading: 1 Samuel 30; John 11:25–35

Grateful Praise

*"Then David and all the house of Israel played music before the
Lord on all kinds of instruments of fir wood, on harps, on
stringed instruments, on tambourines, on sistrums,
and on cymbals." 2 Samuel 6:5*

As a teenager, I was always fascinated by personality quizzes
and inventories. Now as a mother, it has been interesting for me
to reflect on my parenting style. How do your deepest held beliefs
about the office of parenthood affect the way you practice
discipling your children? Whether your personal parenting style is
more authoritative or permissive, there's something we could all
use a little bit more of in our parenting: praise!

It's not difficult to get caught up in all there is to "do" as a
mother: not just cooking, laundry, and dishes, but also teaching
your children to develop character. It's so easy to fall into a
pattern of nagging your children to get their chores done, their
homework done, and their growing-up done. It's so easy to fall
into a pattern of daily frustration and disregard for all of the
blessings God so richly pours upon us.

Take some time today, every day, every hour, to reflect on the
Lord's rich mercies to you and your family. He pours His
forgiveness on us, washing away our spirit of ungratefulness and
nagging, and giving us a joyful heart of praise!

*For the joy of human love,
Brother, sister, parent, child;
Friends on earth, and friends above,
Pleasures pure and undefiled:
Lord of all, to Thee we raise
This our hymn of grateful praise. (463:3)*

For Further Reading: 2 Samuel 6; Psalm 100

Sweet Sleep

"I lay down and slept; I awoke, for the Lord sustained me....I will both lie down in peace, and sleep; For You alone, O Lord, make me dwell in safety." Psalms 3:5, 4:8

Whatever feeling is deep in your heart, you'll find it expressed somewhere in the psalms. David, Solomon, Asaph (one of David's three choir leaders), the Sons of Korah (the Levitical choir in the temple), and others wrote these wonderful lyrics inspired by God. They were the hymns of the Old Testament, the hymns our Savior would have sung and memorized as a boy.

In your vocation as a mother, you have a myriad of responsibilities, much to be concerned about. Maybe those never-ending duties keep you up at night. Or perhaps you have no trouble falling asleep: it's the near-impossible rising in the morning that you find disheartening, yet another day of repetition and thanklessness.

Take comfort that our Savior, too, was a human like you, but sinless. Jesus needed rest, just like you. Because He took on flesh, He felt our exhaustion. He isn't a God faraway, but present at each moment—both falling asleep and rising. For those who have trouble falling asleep, He knows our troubles and worries intimately. For those who have trouble waking and getting up, He's felt the same bone-weary exhaustion. Trust in His unfailing love to calm the waves of your heart.

Teach me to live that I may dread
The grave as little as my bed.
Teach me to die that so I may
Rise glorious at the awe-full Day.
O may my soul on Thee repose,
And may sweet sleep mine eyelids close,
Sleep that shall me more vig'rous make
To serve my God when I awake! (565:2)

For Further Reading: Psalms 3 and 4; Mark 4:35–41

And Should My Heart for Sorrow Break

*"I am weary with my groaning; All night I make my bed swim;
I drench my couch with my tears....You number my wanderings;
Put my tears into Your bottle; Are they not in Your book?"*
Psalms 6:6, 56:8

Who knows you best? Your husband, perhaps? Your best friend? Your mother? Even your loved ones who are intimately acquainted with you are not privy to the number of tears you've cried. But God is. He knows each and every one. He's bottled them up and recorded your sorrows and longings in His book.

Any woman worth her weight in estrogen has cried. Probably even "ugly" cried. We may grieve legitimately for the pain and loss of others in our lives. We might weep out of selfishness, for our own lost dreams and desires. Sometimes, we even cry wishing to give up our vocation as a mother, because it just seems too hard.

But our groanings are not lost on God. Though His answers to our prayers may not be what we want, He always hears us. He knows. You are never alone in your hurt, whatever the cause. What a precious reminder that David records of God's omnipresent love for us sinners!

*Lord, Thee I love with all my heart;
I pray Thee, ne'er from me depart;
With tender mercy cheer me.
Earth has no pleasure I would share,
Yea, heav'n itself were void and bare
If Thou, Lord, were not near me.
And should my heart for sorrow break,
My trust in Thee no one could shake.
Thou art the Portion I have sought;
Thy precious blood my soul has bought.
Lord Jesus Christ,
My God and Lord, my God and Lord,
Forsake me not! I trust Thy Word. (406:1)*

For Further Reading: Psalms 6 and 56; Isaiah 53:1–6

The Incarnation

"But You are He who took Me out of the womb; You made Me
trust while on My mother's breasts. I was cast upon You from
birth. From My mother's womb You have been My God."
Psalm 22:9–10

There are many different ways to classify individual psalms. There are psalms of lament, judgment, thanksgiving, and history. There are psalms specifically created to be used in worship. There are also several Messianic psalms, in which God uses David to look forward to the coming Savior and prophesy of His life. Psalm 22 is a Messianic psalm.

In the verses above, David was not only expressing a human truth: that each and every human was planned and created by God, but also that our Savior Himself would grow within Mary's womb and nurse at her breast. It is a precious blessing to be reassured that each of our children is treasured by the Creator as an individual person. But what an abundantly greater blessing to know that, to save sinners, becoming a human Himself was not too great of a humility for Christ!

Interestingly, the authors of the People's Bible Commentary of Matthew speculate that this passage, this Psalm, and perhaps even Psalms 1–23 were recited by Jesus on the cross and gave Him comfort during His last hours. The first verse of Psalm 22 is one of the words of Jesus on the cross, "My God, My God, why have you forsaken Me." No answer to that question is given directly by the Father, but Jesus would have received comfort by reciting to the end of this psalm, "[God] has not hidden His face, but has listened to his cry for help!" What comfort for each Christian, each mother!

> *He nestles at His mother's breast,*
> *Receives her tender care,*
> *Whom angels hail with joy most blest,*
> *King David's royal Heir, King David's royal Heir. (148:4)*

For Further Reading: Psalm 22; Mark 15:27–39

Create In Me

"Behold, I was brought forth in iniquity, And in sin my mother conceived me....Create in me a clean heart, O God, And renew a steadfast spirit within me....A broken and a contrite heart—These, O God, You will not despise." Psalm 51:5,10,17

"You are the man!" the Prophet Nathan accused the king. David was the man who had stolen a precious lamb (Bathsheba) from a poor man (Uriah, her husband) in the prophet's parable. The king had Uriah killed in order to disguise his own sin.

Confronted with his wickedness, David confessed, "I have sinned against the Lord." While the king's conduct is nothing to be emulated, his confession was heartfelt, and an example to all Christians caught in sin (2 Sam. 12). Reflecting on this incident, David pens Psalm 51, begging God not to look upon his sins, but to change him from the inside out.

Each of us, each of our children, was born from a body which carried the sin of our first parents, Adam and Eve. There is nothing good in us which longs for God or chooses Him. God works that change within us. Christ was born without iniquity to redeem all conceived in sin. Praise the Lord that just as He cleaned and renewed David, in Christ, He cleans and renews you, gifting the Holy Spirit, and equipping you to know and do His will each day.

*Though alive, I'm dead in sin, Lost to all good things by nature.
Holy Ghost, change me within,
Make of me a newborn creature;
For the flesh works ruination
And can never gain salvation.
All desire and thoughts of mine From my youth are only evil.
Save me by Thy pow'r divine
From myself and from the devil;
Give me strength in ample measure
Both to will and do Thy pleasure. (220:2,4)*

For Further Reading: Psalm 51; Romans 7:13–25

A Mansion with the Blest!

"But now he is dead; why should I fast? Can I bring him back again? I shall go to him, but he shall not return to me."
2 Samuel 12:23

After I experienced a miscarriage, a woman at church attempted to give me comfort about "losing a child." My oldest daughter overheard this conversation and later asked me, "Mama, the baby isn't really lost at all, right? The baby is in Heaven, in God's hands. We all know where it is."

Have you experienced the "loss" of a child? Are you prepared to, if that day comes in the future? No one wants to dwell on the possibility of the death of her child, or on the possibility of her own death. But in fact, we do consider the afterlife weekly in our worship services during the creed: "I acknowledge one baptism for the remission of sins, And I look for the Resurrection of the dead and the Life of the world to come. Amen."

You are ready. Your children are ready. They have been bought with the precious blood of Jesus and bear His name on their foreheads and breast. We know that the end of life on earth is not the end of life. Any babies who have gone before us—having heard God's Word, being grafted into His vine—any Christian loved ones rest, waiting for us in the mansion of Heaven.

> *Brief life is here our portion;*
> *Brief sorrow, short-lived care;*
> *The life that knows no ending,*
> *The tearless life, is there.*
> *O happy retribution:*
> *Short toil, eternal rest;*
> *For mortals and for sinners*
> *A mansion with the blest! (534:3)*

For Further Reading: 2 Samuel 12; 1 Corinthians 15:12–28

Flooded by Emotion

"Save me, O God! For the waters have come up to my neck. I sink in deep mire, Where there is no standing; I have come into deep waters, Where the floods overflow me." Psalm 69:1–2

As I write this devotion, Houston, Texas, is under water from Hurricane Harvey. The photos I have seen picture devastation, utter destruction. Hopefully few women reading these devotions will experience this level of physical ruination in their lives. But almost all of us have experienced some level of emotional ravage.

In this psalm of David, physical drowning is pictured as a metaphor for utter emotional grief. The trials, frustrations, and responsibilities of motherhood can leave us paralyzed, frozen in the deep waters, unable to pull ourselves out. We sputter for air, craning our necks, to get our nostrils just past the surface of the rising flood.

Paradoxically, though, it is by a flood you are lifted out of the muck and mire! By the blood and water poured from Jesus' side on your behalf, you are saved. When that water is sprinkled on us in baptism, when we drink that very blood in the Lord's Supper, He pours out that flood again. When you feel yourself drowning in a flood of sorrows, remember Christ's own blood—a flood for you. (Notice the shape of the chalice in the hymn below.)

> *Alleluia! Let praises ring!*
> *Unto the Lamb of God we sing,*
> *In whom we are elected.*
> *He bought His Church with His own blood,*
> *He cleansed her in that blessed flood,*
> *And as His Bride selected.*
> *Holy, Holy*
> *Is our union*
> *And communion.*
> *His befriending*
> *Gives us joy and peace unending. (6:2)*

For Further Reading: Psalm 69; John 19:34

The Angel Band

"For He shall give His angels charge over you, To keep you in all your ways. In their hands they shall bear you up, Lest you dash your foot against a stone." Psalm 91:11–12

When I was a little girl, I loved to ride my bike around the neighborhood. Once, I planned a U-turn, but failed to first look over my shoulder. I turned directly into an oncoming car, just feet from a head-on collision. In front of my face, I miraculously saw the laws of physics defied: instantaneously, my momentum changed direction and I was pushed out of the way of the vehicle. I can only attribute the experience to God's providence and guardian angels.

While you may not have had such a dramatic "angelic" encounter, what a comfort it is to know that God gives us the gift of this protection, day and night! While sometimes our earthly impressions of angels include "cute little cherubs," Scripture describes them as mighty soldiers or warriors—angels constantly have to reassure humans to " fear not" when they bring messages!

Angels are sent by God to our children, too. Mothers can't always be near to protect them as they age; even when we are around, sometimes we are helpless. We pray with Luther, "Into Your hands I commend myself, my body and soul and all things. Let Your holy angel be with me." God alone knows the time appointed to bring us to eternal life. Until then, praise be to Him for His gift of the angels to keep our children safe!

> *But watchful is the angel band*
> *That follows Christ on ev'ry hand*
> *To guard His people where they go*
> *And break the counsel of the foe.*
> *And thus our God, still at this day,*
> *From harm and many an evil way*
> *Keeps us by His dear angel guard,*
> *Placed over us as watch and ward. (545:7,10)*

For Further Reading: Psalms 91 and 34:6–8

The Ministry of Reconciliation

"The Lord is merciful and gracious, Slow to anger, and abounding in mercy....He has not dealt with us according to our sins, Nor punished us according to our iniquities.... As far as the east is from the west, So far has He removed our transgressions from us." Psalm 103:8,10,12

"Mom is merciful and gracious, slow to anger and abounding in mercy!" What I wouldn't give for my kids to think of me thus! If they said the exact opposite, it would be closer to the truth! Not only do I become upset at my children so quickly, I often find myself holding a grudge against them, even after they've apologized and I've "said" that I forgive them. This rhetoric also applies to the attitudes I frequently see displayed among siblings. Psalm 133 states how beautiful it is when brothers dwell together in unity! From the sound of the arguing in the bedroom beneath my computer, unity is the farthest thing from their minds!

With all of this frustration, can this really be a Christian home? Yes! Luther says, "A Christian is not someone who has no sin; he is someone to whom, because of his faith in Christ, God does not impute his sin" (*Luther's Works* 26:133). We know and feel these shortcomings in our hearts. And that's why this psalm offers us such sweet comfort! Our failures, our children's failures, are gone—crucified to the cross! Christ has reconciled us to God and to one another. Even during brief (or ongoing) unrest in our home, we remain God's forgiven children.

May God bestow on us His grace and favor
To please Him with our behavior
And live as brethren here in love and union
Nor repent this blest Communion!
O Lord, have mercy!
Let not Thy good Spirit forsake us;
Grant that heav'nly-minded He make us;
Give Thy Church, Lord, to see Days of peace and unity:
O Lord, have mercy! (327:3)

For Further Reading: Psalm 103; 2 Corinthians 5:17–21

A Heritage

"Behold, children are a heritage from the Lord, The fruit of the womb is a reward. Like arrows in the hand of a warrior, So are the children of one's youth. Happy is the man who has his quiver full of them....Your wife shall be like a fruitful vine In the very heart of your house, Your children like olive plants All around your table. Behold, thus shall the man be blessed Who fears the Lord." Psalms 127:3–5, 128:3–4

The rhetoric of the world constantly bombards us with messages contrary to the Word of God. The burden of children is an especially strong deception in our culture. But, it is also ingrained in our selfish sinful nature: How many of us are fearful of another child? Is there any mention of children as burdens in the verses above? God clearly paints children as blessings, a source of deep happiness—the only earthly gift that can also be taken to Heaven!

Is it any wonder, though, that Satan, the world, and our flesh desire to deceive us about the truth of the blessing of children? We know from Psalm 78 that the next generation, our children and their children, is an evangelism tool God uses to spread the faith! What a precious heritage God has given us, both in our children and in the task of bringing future generations to the knowledge of the Lord. "For the promise [of forgiveness] is to you and to your children, and to all who are afar off, as many as the Lord our God will call" (Acts 2:39). His strength emboldens us for this task.

> *God's grace alone endureth,*
> *And children's children yet shall prove*
> *How He with strength assureth*
> *The hearts of all that seek His love.*
> *In heav'n is fixed His dwelling; His rule is over all.*
> *Angels, in might excelling, Bright hosts, before Him fall.*
> *Praise Him who ever reigneth, All ye who hear His Word.*
> *Nor our poor hymns disdaineth—My soul, O bless the Lord! (456:4)*

For Further Reading: Psalms 127 and 128; Psalm 37

Marvelous Are Your Works!

*"For You formed my inward parts; You covered me in my
mother's womb. I will praise You, for I am fearfully and
wonderfully made; Marvelous are Your works, And that my soul
knows very well. My frame was not hidden from You,
When I was made in secret....Your eyes saw my substance, being
yet unformed. And in Your book they all were written, The days
fashioned for me, When as yet there were none of them."
Psalm 139:13–16*

How easy it is to get caught up in our daily frustrations with
our children! As imperfect mothers, we wonder why our son just
can't "get it" or why our daughter always acts "like that." We
sometimes get stuck in our perceptions, whether or not they are
grounded in reality. Sure, our children are sinners with
shortcomings and failings (just like Mom), but they are also
fearfully and wonderfully made (just like Mom)!

Remember the moment you found yourself pregnant with
that frustrating child? Whether that instant was filled with joy or
fear, it was humbling. To know that God is using a simple, sinful
vessel—namely, you—to knit together new life is astounding! The
child is totally dependent on you, and yet you have no control over
the outcome of the pregnancy! Job 34 puts it well: "If [God]
should gather to Himself...His breath, All flesh would perish
together, And man would return to dust." Both before and after
their births, our children are precious lives belonging to God and
redeemed by Him. (Their mothers are, too.) Each of our days is
ordained by Him, including the challenging days of motherhood.

*Praise to the Lord,
who hath fearfully, wondrously, made thee;
Health hath vouchsafed
and, when heedlessly falling, hath stayed thee.
What need or grief Ever hath failed of relief?
Wings of His mercy did shade thee. (65:3)*

For Further Reading: Psalm 139; Job 10:8–12

Praying Our Complaints

"I pour out my complaint before Him; I declare before Him my trouble....To all who call upon Him in truth. He will fulfill the desire of those who fear Him; He also will hear their cry and save them." Psalms 142:2, 145:18–19

I have to admit it: by (sinful) nature, I'm a complainer. When my husband comes home from work and asks how my day went, I usually tell him everything that went wrong! How about you? Are you a complainer? When the toddler is naughty, or the teen is negligent, do you call a friend and grumble? Do you fuss when something in your home goes wrong? Well, what's a mom to do about it, besides complain? How about pray!?

In Psalms 142 and 145, under inspiration, David tells us to Whom we should complain. God is listening! He's given us the warning of the Israelites complaining in the wilderness; this temptation came from Satan, and destroyed them (1 Cor. 10:10)! But Paul, in his letter to the Philippian church, echoes the psalmist's sentiment, "But in everything by prayer and supplication, with thanksgiving, let your requests be made known to God" (4:6). Our faithful Father knows our troubles and hears our cries. He sent our Lord Jesus to wash away your heart of complaint and give you a spirit of contentment. Peace flows from bringing our complaints to our Savior, not by sharing them with the world. What promises and blessings result when we hold up our complaints to the Hearer in prayer!

> *Lord, You know best my needs,*
> *My pains You're sharing;*
> *Your Word and grace now feeds*
> *The lamb You're bearing.*
> *What more could I desire with You deciding*
> *The course which I now take?*
> *I follow in the wake*
> *Where You are guiding! (83:5)*

For Further Reading: Psalms 142 and 145; Philippians 4:4–9

Solomon's Prayer, and Ours

"Your servant is in the midst of Your people whom You have chosen, a great people, too numerous to be numbered or counted. Therefore give to Your servant an understanding heart to judge Your people, that I may discern between good and evil. For who is able to judge this great people of Yours?" 1 Kings 3:8–9

After the death of his father, Solomon went to Gibeon and sacrificed one thousand animals to the Lord. God was pleased with his action, and came to Solomon in a dream, inquiring about the greatest desire of Solomon's heart. Solomon replied to the Lord with the Scripture passage above.

How much like our own mother's heart is Solomon's prayer! Do you feel humbled by the awesome responsibility of raising your children for the Lord? Do you feel inadequate for the task before you? Do you feel frustration at your own lack of resources? You should, for of yourself, you are ill-equipped for any good work, much less the all-important work of imparting the faith to your children. Still, our Heavenly Father places these children into our arms and our homes. God Himself in the person of Christ has forgiven all of our mothering blunders. Daily, we can call on the Merciful One to strengthen us. We pray, "I am in the midst of Your people whom You have chosen. Therefore give to me an understanding heart to care for Your people, that I may discern between good and evil. For who is able to care for this people of Yours?" Rest assured, Solomon's King hears your prayers and will equip you each day.

> *With one accord, O God, we pray:*
> *Grant us Thy Holy Spirit.*
> *Look Thou on our infirmity*
> *Through Jesus' blood and merit.*
> *Grant us to grow in grace each day*
> *By holy baptism that we may*
> *Eternal life inherit! (241:2)*

For Further Reading: 1 Samuel 3; John 14:15–27

Expecting Perfection?

"When they sin against You (for there is no one who does not sin)
...and repent, and make supplication to You...and when they
return to You with all their heart and with all their soul... forgive
Your people who have sinned against You, and all their
transgressions which they have transgressed against You;
and grant them compassion." 1 Kings 8:46–48,50

Most Christian moms know the formula: After disciplining a child, he or she ought to apologize and you ought to forgive. But, after this takes place, it seems that both mother and child experience amnesia. The child forgets that a key piece of repentance is turning from sin, and the mother forgets that the child in her care is all the while sinner while also saint.

Why are we disgusted and appalled when our children sin, as if we expect perfection? On the one hand, we do anticipate perfection from our children, much like God demands it from us. On the other hand, we as corrupt mothers hold the bar awfully high for our own sinful progeny! The key difference between a mother's assumptions and God's demands is that God Himself meets the expectation He requires by cleansing us in the blood of Jesus.

Of our own merits, neither we nor our children can ever meet God's standards. We need His forgiveness and restoration again and again, just as Solomon recognized at the dedication of the temple. Only when we recognize how much we've truly been given—Christ's perfection—can we whole-heartedly forgive our own children when they fail to meet our expectations.

Forgive me, O Lord,
My sins and transgressions in deed and in word!
Thou knowest my heart and my innermost thought,
The words I have spoken, the deeds I have wrought,
My errors and failings I deeply abhor,
Forgive and restore, Forgive and restore! (575:3)

For Further Reading: 1 Kings 8; Matthew 18:21–35

Self-Help?

"Blessed be the Lord your God, who delighted in you, setting you on the throne of Israel! Because the Lord has loved Israel forever, therefore He made you king, to do justice and righteousness." 1 Kings 10:9

In a devotion book written by a woman, for women, it's nice to include a few quotations by women from the Bible! In the passage above, the Queen of Sheba speaks these words to King Solomon after coming for a visit to Jerusalem. She's impressed after receiving a tour of his home and riches. She's even more impressed by the gift of Solomon's wisdom. She herself is wise, for she recognized God's gift of wisdom in His servant, the king.

While Solomon is well-known as the "wisest man who ever lived," even he was lured into sin. It wasn't his wisdom that blessed him or saved him; it was the Lord, the God of Israel. Where do you look for wisdom? If you look to yourself, you will be sorely disappointed, for certainly your own wisdom cannot rival that of the sinful "wisest man" on earth, or probably even the wisdom of the Queen of Sheba. When we look for wisdom about how to deal with sin in our families and dwell in peace, the only authentic "self-help" comes from outside of ourselves!

The story of Scripture is not meant to be a parenting handbook; it is the story of humanity's salvation by grace through faith in the Messiah. Yet, its Writer is wise from eternity. He has so much wisdom for families, mothers, and children. Let's open our Bibles and read, gaining His wisdom, putting it into practice by the power of the Holy Spirit.

> *Nothing in my hand I bring,*
> *Simply to Thy cross I cling;*
> *Naked, come to Thee for dress,*
> *Helpless, look to Thee for grace.*
> *Foul, I to the fountain fly—*
> *Wash me, Savior, or I die! (286:3)*

For Further Reading: 1 Kings 10; Romans 11:33

Little Moochers

"Do not say to your neighbor, 'Go, and come back, And tomorrow I will give it,' When you have it with you." Prov. 3:28

This proverb is highlighted in my Bible from my days of dorm living, with a scrawled note: "Moochers!" Apparently, "mooching" in the dorms was a common problem! Fast forward a few decades, and many days I feel like my own children are mooching from me —if not from my things, from my time!

So often, we try to teach our children, our closest little neighbors, not to be selfish, to share generously. But we have a difficult time modeling this ourselves! Let's face it: kids can ruin our stuff, our plans. Many times, we resist sharing with them, either physically or emotionally, putting off their desires indefinitely. Solomon reminds us not to put off fulfilling the requests of our neighbor.

In the parable of the Good Samaritan, Jesus answers both the question of "Who is my neighbor" and also "How can I serve that neighbor?" Both those closest to us and our enemies are our neighbors. Unfortunately, we fall far short of the example of the Good Samaritan, often passing by our children's requests. However, Jesus is our perfect neighbor, our perfect brother, caring for us with His charity, even to the point of giving His life. What hope and comfort we have because of His forgiveness! Because we have been filled with Love, we can serve our little neighbors with selflessness.

> *Wondrous honor hast Thou given*
> *To our humblest charity*
> *In Thine own mysterious sentence,*
> *"Ye have done it unto Me."*
> *Can it be, O gracious Master,*
> *Thou dost deign for alms to sue,*
> *Saying by Thy poor and needy,*
> *"Give as I have giv'n to you"? (459:3)*

For Further Reading: Proverbs 3; Luke 10:25–37

Get Wisdom!

"When I was my father's son, Tender and the only one in the sight of my mother, He also taught me, and said to me: 'Let your heart retain my words; Keep my commands, and live. Get wisdom! Get understanding! Do not forget, nor turn away from the words of my mouth.'...Wisdom is the principal thing; Therefore get wisdom. And in all your getting, get understanding." Proverbs 4:3–5,7

Even aside from extra-curricular activities, life with children is busy! Whether kissing boo-boos or filling out the FAFSA, life with children never slows down! And yet, Solomon reminds us of a critical aspect of parenting: teaching our children wisdom. Is this on your "to-do" list?

True wisdom is found by studying God's Word and learning of His love and forgiveness in Christ; that can never be crossed off of your "to-do" list! So often, Bible study is the first thing to be neglected from our schedules when we are busy. Indeed, it can be overwhelming to even know where to start looking for wisdom. James 1:5 gives mothers some inspired advice, "If any of you lacks wisdom, you should ask God, who gives generously to all without finding fault, and it will be given to you" (NIV).

Some scholars believe that Wisdom is personified as Jesus in the Scriptures. The reason we are forgiven for not pursuing Heavenly wisdom as our mothering priority is Wisdom Himself! This paradox inspires us to pursue Scripture no matter how busy!

Blessed is the man that never
Doth in godless counsel meet;
Nor in sinners' way stands ever,
Nor sits in the scorner's seat,
But on God's all-perfect law
Meditates with holy awe;
Day and night he delves for treasure
In the Word—'tis all his pleasure. (457:1)

For Further Reading: Psalm 1; Proverbs 4

Listening to Advice

"Give instruction to a wise man, and he will be still wiser....
Whoever loves instruction loves knowledge, But he who hates
correction is stupid....He who disdains instruction despises his
own soul, But he who heeds rebuke gets understanding."
Proverbs 9:9, 12:1, 15:32

It wasn't many days into my mothering career when I was offered advice by my own parents. It was sound advice, but at the time, it made me prickle! This was *my* child! This was *my* decision. Why should *anyone*, even my wise parents, question *my* wisdom? Over the years, my own philosophies have failed and I have been thoroughly humbled. I am still learning to consider the well-intentioned advice of others, especially Biblical wisdom, rather than feeling offense when it is offered—even the parenting advice offered by my own kids!

Humility is part of our Christian walk. "No man can be thoroughly humbled until he knows that his salvation is utterly beyond his own powers, devices, endeavors, will and works, and depends entirely on the choice, will, and work of another, namely, of God alone" (*Luther's Works*, 33:62). Our own parenting wisdom cannot save us! Putting aside our pride can be a challenge, but our Savior is no stranger to humility. Having taken on flesh, He humbled Himself and became obedient to the point of death. He has taken your pride onto Himself. When God looks at you, He sees Christ's humility.

> *For my proud and haughty spirit*
> *Thy humiliation paid;*
> *For my death Thy death and merit*
> *Have a full atonement made:*
> *Thy reproaches and dishonor*
> *All have tended to my honor:*
> *Thousand, thousand thanks to Thee,*
> *Blessed Jesus, ever be! (336:4)*

For Further Reading: Proverbs 9, 12, and 15; Philippians 2:5–11

Words of Love

"The mouth of the righteous is a well of life, But violence covers the mouth of the wicked....A soft answer turns away wrath, But a harsh word stirs up anger....A wholesome tongue is a tree of life." Proverbs 10:11, 15:1,4

How do you do with speaking words of love toward your children? At best, I can go for hours, but sometimes only minutes, without "violence" proceeding from my mouth! Before long, I always fall back into the same old wicked words. I've read James 1:19–20 so many times: "Let every man be swift to hear, slow to speak, slow to wrath; for the wrath of man does not produce the righteousness of God." I stand convicted, confessing that I have sinned so often with negative words to my family.

Yes, God desires that we speak words of love to our children. And yet, even when we fail, Jesus speaks His words of love to us: "God so loved the world that He gave His only begotten Son, that whoever believes in Him should not perish but have everlasting life. For God did not send His Son into the world to condemn the world, but that the world through Him might be saved" (John 3:16–17). While you dwell here on earth, battles with your tongue will be ongoing, and your children have inherited those battles. But God's Word of love is more powerful than the human tongue.

So let your tongue, your heart, and mind
Agree to banish ev'ry kind
Of malice, falsehood and disguise,
And here on earth a paradise
Of peace and harmony maintain,
Where concord and good will shall reign.
For God observes our thoughts and deeds,
The secrets of our heart He reads;
The wicked cannot be concealed,
Their evil ways shall be revealed,
He ev'ry true believer knows,
And love and grace on him bestows. (418:4,5)

For Further Reading: Proverbs 10 and 15; 1 John 4:7–12

Practicing Patience

"A fool's wrath is known at once, But a prudent man covers shame....The discretion of a man makes him slow to anger, And his glory is to overlook a transgression." Proverbs 12:16, 19:11

A modern proverb quips that if a woman prays for more patience, she should be ready to receive plenty of practice in the form of difficulties! Doesn't every mother wish for more patience? And surely the Lord has provided ample practice!

Jesus had plenty of opportunities to practice patience while He lived on earth. He endured seemingly endless questions from His confused disciples. He experienced hoards of hungry crowds needing to be fed. He encountered countless people with sickness and disease, healing many. Even during his last 24 hours of earthly life, our Lord modeled true patience. Though oppressed and afflicted at His trial, He didn't lose His patience or demand justice. He didn't assert His rightful power and authority. He didn't convict His hearers of their inconceivable sin, namely sentencing God to death. Instead, He kept silent, like a lamb led to the sacrifice.

Bearing the sins of all humanity, including your sins of impatience, Christ kept silent: not just once, but three times prior to His crucifixion—before the Sanhedrin, Pilate, and Herod (see Mark 14:60–61, John 19:8–11, and Luke 23:9). May our precious Savior grant us a measure of His patience, and an equal measure of His silence, as needed! May mothers everywhere be a reflection of God's grace to those around them, regardless of their personal circumstances or individual trials.

> *Help me speak what's right and good*
> *And keep silence on occasion.*
> *Help me pray, Lord, as I should,*
> *Help me bear my tribulation.*
> *Help me die and let my spirit*
> *Everlasting life inherit. (220:8)*

For Further Reading: Proverbs 12 and 19; Isaiah 53:7–12

Chastisement

"He who spares his rod hates his son, But he who loves him disciplines him promptly....Chasten your son while there is hope, And do not set your heart on his destruction....Correct your son, and he will give you rest; Yes, he will give delight to your soul."
Proverbs 13:24, 19:18, 29:17

When you notice bickering or misbehavior in your kids, what's your first reaction? I usually think, "Seriously? Do I really need to get off the couch *again*?" Instead, I should be contemplating the blessing it is that I have children to bring up in the nurture and admonition of the Lord.

Why is it that we dislike disciplining our children? Why are we so lazy that we often avoid it? For me, I know it is bothersome because I perceive discipline as an interruption to my own plans, rather than a part of my routine. Discipline also brings up unpleasant memories from my childhood. Am I being too harsh or too lenient? I constantly second-guess myself.

The Hebrew word for "chasten" or "correct" used in the passages above doesn't necessarily indicate physical punishment; it specifically means "instruction" or "correction." How often mothers fail to do this act of love for our children, setting them on the right path and giving spiritual instruction, instead hoping the issue will resolve itself.

Our Heavenly Father has not neglected His fatherly duty toward us. The Lord disciplines those He loves. True, it isn't pleasant at the time, but it yields important fruit. Times of uncertainty regarding the discipline of our children will still remain on earth, but what a comfort to know that God forgives us for all of our sins, both of harshness and leniency in discipline.

(O for a faith...) That will not murmur nor complain
Beneath the chast'ning rod,
But in the hour of grief or pain Will lean upon its God. (364:2)

For Further Reading: Proverbs 13, 19, and 29; Hebrews 12:3–11

Heavenly Treasures

"Better is a little with the fear of the Lord, Than great treasure with trouble....Give me neither poverty nor riches—Feed me with the food allotted to me; Lest I be full and deny You, And say, 'Who is the Lord?' Or lest I be poor and steal, And profane the name of my God." Proverbs 15:16, 30:8–9

Economics experts preach that a child will cost parents hundreds of thousands of dollars during their first 18 years of life. And that doesn't even include private schooling or college! No wonder so many parents feel they cannot afford more children!

What the experts don't explain, though, is that children don't *have* to cost that much! And in fact, God calls children themselves blessings, not burdens. Whether you are caring for one child, or a dozen, finances can certainly be a stressor. However, if your budget is tight, consider that God may be helping your children grow in Godly character and appreciate life with less. It's okay if you can't provide your children with "fancy" things. In fact, the very thing you lack and perceive as a deficiency may actually have distracted your children from setting their eyes on Heavenly treasures! No one can steal or destroy the spiritual treasures that God has given us and our children through faith in Christ.

We think we know what we need, but the Lord sees our lives clearly; He may protect your family from heartache and strife by *withholding* worldly riches. God provides *in His own way*, not only for this life, but also for the life to come. If He has charted a course for your eternal care through His own life-blood, will He not also care for your earthly needs in the meantime?

> *What is the world to me! My Jesus is my Treasure,*
> *My Life, my Health, my Wealth, My Friend, my Love, my Pleasure,*
> *My Joy, my Crown, my All,*
> *My Bliss eternally.*
> *Once more, then, I declare:*
> *What is the world to me! (446:8)*

For Further Reading: Proverbs 15 and 30; Matthew 6:19–24

ANOTHER Interruption?!

"A man's heart plans his way, But the Lord directs his steps....
There are many plans in a man's heart, Nevertheless the Lord's
counsel—that will stand....A man's steps are of the Lord;
How then can a man understand his own way?"
Proverbs 16:9, 19:21, 20:24

I can hardly believe I'm writing this devotion. I'm a bad person to write it because I hate being interrupted. But even practically speaking, I can't believe I'm writing at all! I've sat down at least a dozen times over the past week to write this very devotion, but have been prevented from it, again and again, due to the needs (and intense wants) of little people in my home.

Every mom knows what it's like to have her plans interrupted. It happens so often, it's actually astounding that we even make plans anymore! But, whatever we might expect from this day, this hour, this moment, God has known from eternity what it would truly hold. It's no surprise for Him. He has prepared, in advance, a good work for us to do: serving our closest neighbor, His children, just as He has served us. When we lose our life (or plans!) for Him, we find what He prepared for us all along (Mark 8:35). Despite any difficult or strenuous change of plans, cling to your Savior and His Word.

> *"Who seeks to save on earth his life*
> *Without Me, he shall lose it:*
> *But who for Me in earthly strife*
> *Now loses it shall find it;*
> *Who counts the cross for Me too hard*
> *Is worthy not of Me, the Lord."*
> *Then let us follow Christ, our Lord,*
> *And take the cross appointed*
> *And, firmly clinging to His Word,*
> *In suff'ring be undaunted.*
> *For all who bear the battle's strain*
> *The crown of life they shall obtain."* (422:5,6)

For Further Reading: Proverbs 16, 19, and 20; Luke 9:23-25

A Gift of God

"He who finds a wife finds a good thing,
And obtains favor from the Lord." Proverbs 18:22

When we think about the gifts God gives us, we often think of earthly blessings: food, shelter, and material goods. We might also reflect on the spiritual blessings He bestows: forgiveness, life, and salvation. But God has given another extremely precious gift to your family that you might not often reflect on: YOU!

Just as a man who finds a wife finds a good thing, a family who has a mother has a good thing. No matter how inadequate you might feel, or how frustrated you may be about situations that seem beyond your control, no matter how "odd or queer" of a mother you might be (Large Catechism, Fourth Commandment), YOU are a gift from God to your family.

What is a gift? It is an undeserved present of love. Does a gift choose itself to be given? No, it is carefully chosen, by a giver who intimately knows the recipient(s). The gift itself is a symbol of affection and care from the person who picked it out. The gift may have no control over to whom it is given, but it is a blessing to whomever receives it.

You are a gift from the Giver to your family. Your worth is not determined by how you act or what you do. You belong to your Heavenly Father; He will use you to serve those in your midst, regardless of your inabilities or unworthiness. In His wisdom, He has perfectly matched you to be the mother of the very children He has given you, flaws and all.

> *O Lord, we come before Thy face;*
> *In ev'ry home bestow Thy grace*
> *On children, father, mother.*
> *Relieve their wants, their burdens ease,*
> *Let them together dwell in peace*
> *And love to one another! (189:4)*

For Further Reading: Proverbs 18 and 31:10–31

Sadness Into Gladness

"Like one who takes away a garment in cold weather,
And like vinegar on soda, Is one who sings songs
to a heavy heart." Proverbs 25:20

What a struggle it can be to see your child suffer grief! Whether the disappointment stems from a bad grade, a broken promise, or the death of a loved one, mothers have an innate desire to fix their children's problems. But sadness itself is not a sin. Even our Savior has been sad. Just like singing an upbeat song can make a depressed person feel isolated, trying to take away sadness can minimize the pain the other person is feeling. It is really much more difficult (and healing) to sit silently and enter into someone else's pain. Job's friends did well at the beginning of the book, when they sat with him in silence (Job 2:13), and they ruined everything when they opened their mouths. Mothers have the privilege of feeling with their children, entering that pain, instead of constantly trying to cheer them up. There's a time for everything, including a time for silence and weeping. In the end, it's not a mother's job to take away sadness; it's God's. He is the One Who will fix everything in the end.

All of our woes, even the childish ones, are the result of sin in the world, one way or another. God comes to us in our pain and weakness; He doesn't shy away. He waits to execute judgment until the Last Day, and while He waits, we will have times of sadness. But, take heart, because the day is coming when God will permanently change our sorrow into singing.

> *Yea, her sins our God will pardon,*
> *Blotting out each dark misdeed;*
> *All that well deserved His anger*
> *He no more will see or heed.*
> *She hath suffered many a day;*
> *Now her griefs have passed away.*
> *God will change her pining sadness*
> *Into ever-springing gladness. (102:2)*

For Further Reading: Proverbs 25; Ecclesiastes 3:1–7

Executor of Justice

"Speak up for those who cannot speak for themselves, for the rights of all who are destitute." Proverbs 31:8 (NIV)

Before I was a mom, I never anticipated how much my job-title would include "referee" and "arbitrator." How often our children fight with one another! How often one (or more) claims to have been wronged! As mothers, we are called to be an "executor of justice" for our children, defending little ones who have no recourse against the evil done to them. But, we're also warned in Scripture to show mercy and compassion to the perpetrators, as well (Micah 6:8; Zech. 7:9).

It's a difficult balance to strike. Sometimes we neglect justice, hoping the argument will work itself out without our intervention. Sometimes we don't take the time to listen, punishing the wrong party. We desire to execute justice, but also mercy; and yet, rarely does everyone seem satisfied in the end. On this side of Heaven, it seems we fail at this role altogether! We'll never get it right!

However, our Judge, our High Priest, understands our difficulty! Christ was tempted in all points, just as we are, and yet, was without sin. Let us go boldly before our King's throne and find His grace and mercy as the ultimate Executor of Justice (Heb. 4:15–16)! You are justified by Him for all your vocational failings, for all the times you have not spoken up for those who cannot speak for themselves. God cannot pervert justice (Job 34:12), executing that demand onto His undeserving Son in your place. Now, He is free to shower both you and your children with His abundant mercy.

> *He fills the poor with good;*
> *He gives the suff'rers rest:*
> *The Lord hath judgments for the proud*
> *And justice for th'opprest. (60:5)*

For Further Reading: Proverbs 31:1-9; Romans 3:20–26

Genealogy

"Adam, Seth, Enosh, Cainan, Mahalalel, Jared, Enoch,
Methuselah, Lamech, Noah, Shem, Ham, and Japheth....
And Azel had six sons whose names were these:
Azrikam, Bocheru, Ishmael, Sheariah, Obadiah, and Hanan;
these were the sons of Azel." 1 Chronicles 1:1, 9:44

Nine whole chapters, filled with name after name after name! Surely God didn't include this genealogy just to fill the Bible with potential baby-name material! No, these chapters of Scripture chronicle the "ripple-effect" of fathers discipling (or not!) their sons down through the generations. By analogy, the importance of passing on our faith to our children is impressed upon us in a rather chilling way. Our actions (or lack thereof) as parents can affect not just our own babies, but have the potential of affecting great-grandchildren yet unborn. Pretty intimidating, huh?

However, the chronicling of these families goes beyond Adam and Azel, to point us to their most important offspring: these men are the forefathers of the Savior. Beginning at Adam, each of these men sinned, against God, and against their families. From these sinners, the perfect Christ was born. Generations into the future, His perfection penetrates into your life, and by His death and resurrection, Heaven belongs to you! His Spirit enables us to train up the next generation in God's never-ending love, found in that long-awaited Son. His legacy has changed the future of the world, regardless of our own sinful, yet forgiven, deeds.

> *All mankind fell in Adam's fall, One common sin infects us all;*
> *From sire to son the bane descends, And over all the curse impends.*
> *But Christ, the second Adam, came*
> *To bear our sin and woe and shame,*
> *To be our Life, our Light, our Way, Our only Hope, our only Stay.*
> *As by one man all mankind fell And, born in sin, was doomed to hell,*
> *So by one Man, who took our place,*
> *We all received the gift of grace. (491:1,4,5)*

For Further Reading: Matthew 1; 1 Corinthians 15:12–28

God's Many Temples

"Regard the prayer of Your servant and his supplication, O Lord my God, and listen to the cry and the prayer which Your servant is praying before You: that Your eyes may be open toward this temple day and night, toward the place where You said You would put Your name." 2 Chronicles 6:19–20

As wives and mothers, we take pride in the appearance of our homes. We feel good when everything is in its place and the home looks tidy. But, the state of your home isn't always up to you! You have folks in your care with their own thoughts and opinions (or lack thereof!) about the appearance of your home.

Although the prayer of Solomon above is at the dedication of God's house of worship, it's also a prayer we can pray regarding our homes. The most important part of our own dwelling isn't its tidiness, but rather Who dwells within. Our homes are, in a way, the temple of God, His kingdom. From the Second Petition's explanation, we remember, "The kingdom of God comes when our heavenly Father gives us His Holy Spirit, so that by His grace we believe His holy Word and live godly lives here in time and hereafter in eternity." God's gracious eyes are on us and our flock. He has promised to dwell with His children, and has made us just that through baptism. When we read His Word to our children and bring them to church, we hear of his unending love and forgiveness. Our Father strengthens our faith through Jesus' body and blood. Whether your "temple" looks like one or not, rest assured that God has put His name on you in your home and has promised to keep you.

O Lord, let this, Thy little flock, Thy name alone confessing,
Continue in Thy loving care, True unity possessing.
Thy Sacraments, O Lord, And Thy saving Word
To us e'er pure retain.
Grant that they may remain
Our only strength and comfort. (212:2)

For Further Reading: 2 Chronicles 6; 1 Corinthians 6:19–20

Meaningless, Meaningless!

"Then I looked on all the works that my hands had done And on the labor in which I had toiled; And indeed all was vanity and grasping for the wind. There was no profit under the sun."
Ecclesiastes 2:11

A mother's life can seem meaningless, repetitive, dull, and thankless. You probably have similar adjectives bouncing around in your head! The verse above echoes the meaninglessness we sometimes feel with life. However, the writer of these words wasn't a mother. He was a king, and not just any king, but the wisest and richest man on earth at the time. Still, he found the labors of his life to be vanity.

We've all wished our lives could be different somehow...more glamorous, perhaps. Maybe you wish you could be putting your education to "better" use? Perhaps you just desire an exciting change to the daily monotony of housekeeping. Just as children can be thankless about all that their mothers do for them, we can be thankless to our Heavenly Father for all He does for us.

Day in and day out, during the monotony of motherhood or meaninglessness of the monarchy, God is the One Who brings meaning to our lives and redemption to our work. Yes, life this side of Heaven will hold hard work, vain work, that must be done. But, with God's purpose, we look past our light and momentary troubles, to the eternal glory that will someday be revealed in us because of Christ's unfailing love.

I praise for this day
The Father in heaven who prospered my way,
Who shielded from danger, protected from harm,
Promoted my labor, and strengthened my arm;
For hours that passed lightly as birds on the wing,
Thanksgiving I bring, Thanksgiving I bring. (575:3)

For Further Reading: Ecclesiastes 2; 2 Corinthians 4:16–18

True Companionship

"Two are better than one, Because they have a good reward for their labor. For if they fall, one will lift up his companion. Woe to him who is alone when he falls, For he has no one to help him up. Again, if two lie down together, they will keep warm....Though one may be overpowered by another, two can withstand him. And a threefold cord is not quickly broken." Ecclesiastes 4:9–12

Some people have great success finding a spouse through internet dating, but can you imagine finding bosom friends by filling out a survey? The most natural way to find friends is through enjoyable shared experiences! Whether you have one child or twenty, isn't family all about shared experiences? At my wedding, I never would have anticipated that my future children would become my friends; but as we age, I do find joy in their companionship. Of course, there are times when vocation calls for more of an authority figure than a friend, and it can be difficult to discern between the two. However, our children are small reminders of the invisible companionship of our Heavenly Father.

When you reject your children's friendship, you are rejecting God-given companionship. But thankfully, you have a threefold cord, a Friend who sticks closer than a brother (Prov. 18:24), even when you are the opposite of friendly. Jesus calls sinners, even His betrayer, "friend" (Matt. 26:50). Christ demonstrated the greatest love of all by laying down His life for you, His friend, and also your children, your friends (John 15:13).

Let my near and dear ones be
Always near and dear to Thee.
O bring me and all I love
To Thy happy home above.
Jesus, best and kindest Friend,
Thou wilt love me to the end.
Spirit blest, whom I adore,
Let me love Thee more and more. (570:3,5)

For Further Reading: Ecclesiastes 4; Colossians 3:12–14

The Most Incredible Love Story

"I found the one I love. I held him and would not let him go."
Song of Songs 3:4

Likely written by Solomon, the Song of Songs has often been called the greatest love song of all time. Verses alternate between characters: the Beloved, her friends, and the Lover. In the verse above, the Beloved describes her feelings upon finally entering the presence of her true love. Most of us can relate to falling in love with the father of our future children.

This devotion book is about motherhood, not about marital love; however, loving your husband is an often over-looked way of serving your children. Hearken back to that tender time of falling in love and harness it to model a beautiful example for your children.

Marriage isn't always easy. In fact, some readers may be single, separated, or simply struggling in their marriage. We know that no wife or mother is perfect. Even if we hold on to our husband with our actions, sometimes our hearts are elsewhere. But, this is for certain: God has held you, and will not let you go. Christ is the perfect groom; He has washed you clean from all of your marital sins. He woos you to Himself with the most marvelous love song ever composed and places you as the Beloved in the most incredible love story ever conceived.

Serve your husband in your marriage and don't be afraid to let your children see that devotion. But most of all, remember Whose love empowers you to love others as He has loved you.

> *My song is love unknown,*
> *My Savior's love to me,*
> *Love to the loveless shown*
> *That they might lovely be.*
> *O who am I*
> *That for my sake*
> *My Lord should take frail flesh and die? (303:1)*

For Further Reading: Song of Songs; Ephesians 5:22–33

Enough?

"So [the widow of Zarephath]...did according to the word of Elijah; and she and he and her household ate for many days. The bin of flour was not used up, nor did the jar of oil run dry, according to the word of the Lord." 1 Kings 17:15–16

By all earthly calculations, the widow and her son would die. There wasn't more than a bit of food, and now, the prophet was asking her to share? She took him at his word, by faith.

Most of us are not in danger of starving, but we still worry about our daily provisions: food, drink, clothing, shoes, house, home, fields, cattle, money, goods, God-fearing spouse and children, faithful servants and rulers, good government, good weather, peace, health, order, honor, true friends, good neighbors, and the like. Beyond your "daily bread," you might worry if there is "enough" of yourself to go around! Even if you manage to keep food on the table and clothes on the backs of your children, there's always the nagging thought of "enough," especially because you know your own breath will someday run out. What then? Will God provide then?

You can have confidence that, in spite of your failings, death is not the end. Because of Christ's death, death is no longer a punishment for sin, but instead, a glorious doorway into Heaven for the children of God. And while your death may leave behind your family, our omnipotent God will continue to provide for them in your absence. Just as surely as He will raise us up from the dead and give us new and glorious resurrected bodies, He will provide "enough" for our families, day by day, just as He did for the widow and her son.

> *This is the day the Lord hath made,*
> *That all may see His pow'r displayed,*
> *And know His resurrection's pow'r,*
> *To rise by grace and fall no more,*
> *By His own righteousness renewed*
> *And filled with all the life of God. (3:2)*

For Further Reading: 1 Kings 17; Malachi 3:10

Shouts or Whispers?

"[God] said, 'Go out, and stand on the mountain before the Lord.'
And behold, the Lord passed by, and a great and strong wind
tore into the mountains and broke the rocks in pieces before the
Lord, but the Lord was not in the wind; and after the wind an
earthquake, but the Lord was not in the earthquake; and
after the earthquake a fire, but the Lord was not in the fire;
and after the fire a still small voice." 1 Kings 19:11–12

Moms often use the "wind, earthquake, fire" technique when talking to our children. "Perhaps if I raise my voice, they'll listen better?" But, by experience, we know that yelling rarely achieves the desired result. In fact, according to God's example in communicating with the prophet Elijah, the opposite approach—whispering—is more effective! After a yelling episode, moms often commit to improving our approach, but before long, we fall back into our old ways. It's a stark daily example of *simil justus et peccator* (at the same time, saint and sinner). However, whispering isn't the only way God communicates.

In fact, there was a time when Jesus shouted, accompanied by a different earthquake. And God had a pretty important message to share. "Jesus cried out again with a loud voice, and yielded up His spirit. Then, behold, the veil of the temple was torn in two from top to bottom; and the earth quaked" (Mt. 27:50–51). Mothers can aim to stop our yelling, and sometimes, by the power of the Holy Spirit, we'll be successful. But regardless of whether you shout or whisper, Christ's sacrifice for sin is for YOU.

All righteousness by works is vain;
The law brings condemnation.
True righteousness by faith I gain;
Christ's work is my salvation.
His death, that perfect sacrifice,
Has paid the all-sufficient price;
In Him my hope is anchored. (374:4)

For Further Reading: 1 Kings 19; Matthew 27

It Is Well

"[Elisha] said to his servant Gehazi, 'Look, the Shunammite woman! Please run now to meet her, and say to her, "Is it well with you? Is it well with your husband? Is it well with the child?" And she answered, 'It is well.'" 2 Kings 4:25–26

"It is well," the Shunammite woman said. What you don't know, unless you've read the context, is that this woman's long-awaited and earnestly-desired son had just died unexpectedly. The Bible doesn't say she wasn't heartbroken. It doesn't say she knew a miracle was coming her way. It only tells us that though her son had died, it was well with her soul. Oh, for her confession in our own context of unimaginable tragedy!

In the Shunammite woman's case, Elisha returned with her to her home, and by the power of the Almighty, raised her son from the dead. Miracles do happen in this life, and it is right and good for us to seek God's amazing, abundant, and unpredictable power in our own lives. Yet, earthly miracles aside, Christians recognize God's humble, quiet, spiritual miracles: the creation of faith in baptism, the forgiveness of our sins as we eat Christ's body and drink His blood, and the hope He grants, even through tragedy. We also await the ultimate miracle yet to come: the resurrection of the body and an eternity with our Creator.

What was the response of the Shunammite woman after receiving the miracle of life from death? She took her son and went out, living her vocation in praise to the Lord.

> *What God ordains is always good:*
> *This truth remains unshaken.*
> *Though sorrow, need, or death be mine,*
> *I shall not be forsaken.*
> *I fear no harm,*
> *For with His arm*
> *He shall embrace and shield me;*
> *So to my God I yield me. (519:6)*

For Further Reading: 2 Kings 4; John 11:23–27

Rescued!

"Now the Lord had prepared a great fish to swallow Jonah. And Jonah was in the belly of the fish three days and three nights."
Jonah 1:17

Many Bible scholars place the Book of Jonah after the time of Elijah and Elisha. Because the city of Nineveh was thriving during the course of Jonah's history, it is logical to place the events prior to the Babylonians taking over the Assyrian capital city. In addition, Jonah is mentioned in 2 Kings, having preached to King Jeroboam II of Israel (14:25).

Jonah had run away from the Lord's calling, attempting to hide himself from his God-given mission: preaching repentance to a heathen nation. Of course, it's impossible to camouflage oneself from the omniscient, omnipresent Almighty. God will have His way regardless of human inactivity. But, even after Jonah's disobedience, God remains faithful. He rescues the prophet in an unusual way, a way that even today causes Bible-believing Christians to pause. A great fish swallowed Jonah, not to punish him, but to rescue him from drowning!

Whatever the physical needs of your family may be, whatever the spiritual needs of your family may be, remember that God can and does rescue His children in unusual, fantastic, miraculous, and mysterious ways, like a Baby born in a shed and a Man dying on a tree. Like Jonah, call upon Him in your day of trouble and He will rescue you to the glory of His name.

> *God moves in a mysterious way*
> *His wonders to perform;*
> *He plants His footsteps in the sea*
> *And rides upon the storm.*
> *Deep in unknown, unfathomed mines*
> *Of never-failing skill*
> *He treasures up His bright designs*
> *And works His sov'reign will. (434:1)*

For Further Reading: Jonah 1 and 2; Psalm 50:15

Contempt or Compassion?

"And should I [God] not pity Nineveh, that great city, in which are more than one hundred and twenty thousand persons who cannot discern between their right hand and their left—and much livestock?" Jonah 4:11

Jonah, Jonah! His original mission was to preach justice to the pagan city of Nineveh, and they repented! Now, God relented of His anger, and bade Jonah preach of compassion and mercy. At this new assignment, Jonah was disillusioned, self-righteous, and felt sorry for himself. He wanted a different preaching commission altogether! God uses these last words from the Book of Jonah to remind His prophet, and us, of His ultimate purpose: reconciliation with sinners.

Christian mothers rightfully shield their children from the wickedness of the world. But that innocence can sometimes translate into self-righteousness and contempt for the world. While we righteously loathe the world's sin, the Bible never teaches Christ-followers to hate the world's people. Rather, Jesus tells us specifically to love our enemies and pray for them, just as our Heavenly Father cares for their physical needs, even when they refuse to acknowledge Him. If our appearance to unbelievers is hateful, we have made the same mistake Jonah made, assuming others' sins are too far-reaching for God's forgiveness.

The attitude of the world, in general, is to hate Christians, just as Christ is hated by the world. But God would still have us teach our children compassion for unbelievers, continually reflecting His all-redeeming love to the world, to you, to me.

Let the world despise and leave me; They have left my Savior, too.
Human hearts and looks deceive me; Thou art not, like them, untrue.
And while Thou shalt smile upon me,
God of wisdom, love, and might,
Foes may hate and friends may shun me—
Show Thy face, and all is bright. (424:2)

For Further Reading: Jonah 4; Matthew 5:44–46

Slow to Chide and Swift to Bless

"Rend your heart, and not your garments; Return to the Lord your God, For He is gracious and merciful, Slow to anger, and of great kindness; And He relents from doing harm." Joel 2:13

Joel, another prophet of the Lord, foresees the destruction of the Promised Land through a plague of locusts, much like Isaiah will foresee destruction through the Assyrians, and Jeremiah through the Babylonians. However, in the three short chapters of this book, God weaves the lustrous ribbon of His love, as He does throughout the entire tapestry of the Old Testament, renewing His covenant and promise to forgive.

All mothers love their children. Before they are given to us, we envision the beautiful, peaceful, harmonious times of the future. But, once they are in our arms, reality sets in. Things are not perfect. We are not perfect! I didn't know what a temper I had until I was blessed with children!

But God is the perfect Father, and He loves your children far more than you can imagine. He is slow to anger, not wanting any sinner to perish for lack of time to repent! Earlier, Exodus 34 states a comfort similar to the verse above...right after Moses had destroyed the very tablets of the law which God had given him! That is some amazing mercy! He loves each and every one of His children, including you, so much that He would not let your sins separate you from Himself. His faithfulness will not allow Him to do you the harm your mothering failures deserve. Instead, God sent Jesus to atone for your sin and make you perfect in His sight.

Praise Him for His grace and favor
To His people in distress;
Praise Him, still the same forever,
Slow to chide and swift to bless.
Praise Him, praise Him, praise Him, praise Him,
Glorious in His faithfulness. (67:2)

For Further Reading: The Book of Joel; 2 Peter 3:8–9

Judgment and Promise

"Behold, the eyes of the Lord God are on the sinful kingdom,
And I will destroy it from the face of the earth; Yet I will not
utterly destroy the house of Jacob,' Says the Lord." Amos 9:8

Amos's nine chapters are filled with "fire and brimstone." Although he had previously been a shepherd and tree-tender in Judah, God called him to prophesy to the northern tribes of Israel during an era of luxury and opulence. Assyria was coming! Destruction was coming! Doom was coming!

God takes sin seriously. He must punish and destroy it. You and I have the advantage of looking back into the past through God's inspired Word, knowing God has already destroyed our sins on the cross. But, those to whom Amos preached refused God's sacrificial system which foreshadowed the promised Messiah. The God of grace chose here to emphasize His justice and passion against wickedness.

Yet, among these verses foretelling the approaching judgment, there's a hint of mercy: Jacob's children will not be utterly destroyed. God promises to preserve a remnant of faithful believers among the evil in this world: both those who clung to the covenant in Amos's day, and you and your children today.

Presently, our world has the same need for the harsh law, and the sweet Gospel, as it did during Israel's history. Beginning with your own children, may God give you a passion to share the true price of sin, and conversely, the Payment He has sacrificed for justification. Ask the Lord of the Harvest to send out workers, working through you and your children.

> *Thou sacred Love, grace on us bestow,*
> *Set our hearts with heav'nly fire aglow*
> *That with hearts united we love each other,*
> *Of one mind, in peace with ev'ry brother.*
> *Lord, have mercy! (33:3)*

For Further Reading: The Book of Amos; Matthew 9:35–38

Love So Amazing!

"I will have mercy on her who had not obtained mercy; Then I will say to those who were not My people, 'You are My people!' And they shall say, 'You are my God!'" Hosea 2:23

Hosea prophesies in the final days of the Northern Kingdom of Israel, either during the life of Amos, or shortly after. In his book's 14 chapters, God instructs Hosea to take a harlot as his wife, a visual symbol to His people that God had bound Himself to an adulterous and idolatrous race. Hosea was to forgive her continually, a metaphor of Jehovah's everlasting love and forgiveness for His wayward people.

As a woman, as a mother, you have committed the sin of idolatry, just as God's covenant people had. You have placed your own selfish wishes above the needs of those whom God has placed in your care. You have been stubborn and hard of heart when the situation called for tenderness and mercy. You have complained in your heart of your circumstances, jealous for the lives of others. You do not fear, love, and trust in God above all things.

But you remain God's forgiven child, Christ's beloved bride. In one of the most powerful images of the Old Testament, Hosea is commanded to name his third child "Lo-Ammi," translated "not my people" (1:9), driving home the point that Israel's sins separated them from God. But in the reference above, God's overwhelming love and mercy cover Israel's (and your) unfaithfulness. Peter summarizes this in his first epistle, "[You] once were not a people but are now the people of God, who had not obtained mercy but now have obtained mercy" (2:10). You are precious and beloved of the Lord: regardless of your stubbornness or jealousy in the past or present, your future hope is sure.

> *Were the whole realm of nature mine,*
> *That were a tribute far too small;*
> *Love so amazing, so divine,*
> *Demands my soul, my life, my all. (308:4)*

For Further Reading: The Book of Hosea; Romans 9:25–29

The Ultimate Stain Remover

"'Come now, and let us reason together,' Says the Lord,
'Though your sins are like scarlet, They shall be as white as
snow; Though they are red like crimson, They shall be as wool.'"
Isaiah 1:18

The Northern Kingdom (Israel) had been carried off into slavery by Assyria, as foretold by God's prophets. Many events during the Book of Isaiah take place during this time, though it was probably written shortly after the Assyrian army was punished by God. Isaiah also predicts the Babylonian captivity, which would take place over 100 years later. The text is full of frightening judgments, but also rich comfort for those willing to work at reading it. Though an ancient book, Isaiah's words have so much to offer a modern audience.

I don't know much about Isaiah's domestic situation or how often he needed to do laundry, but it seems that he understands a thing or two about garments with stains that need to be scrubbed out. Mothers can relate. Whatever the cause of the stained clothing in our midst, we all know that you can't remove a stain by covering it in blood. But God has ordained spiritual matters to work much differently!

The Judge knows your innermost sins of thought, word, and deed. He sees the unliftable, impenetrable bright red stain of sin that covers you. But ironically, the stain-remover through which God works is blood! Before His crucifixion, Jesus wore a scarlet robe (Mt. 27:28), perhaps symbolic of taking our stains upon Himself. Then, He spilled His blood to wash your heart clean. Now, robed in white, Heaven is yours! Rejoice!

> *O how blest it is to know,*
> *Were as scarlet my transgression,*
> *It shall be as white as snow By Thy blood and bitter Passion,*
> *For these words I now believe—*
> *Jesus sinners doth receive. (426:6)*

For Further Reading: Isaiah 1; Revelation 7:9–14

Before the World About Us

"I will wait on the Lord...I will hope in Him. Here am I and the children whom the Lord has given me! We are for signs and wonders in Israel From the Lord of hosts, Who dwells in Mount Zion." Isaiah 8:17–18

As a mom, I often find myself thinking of my children as a crowd of people instead of as individuals. It is so easy to group the children together, assuming them to be a force for evil ("Those kids are up to it again!"), rather than to see them as individuals with strengths that God is developing to His glory to witness to and serve the world.

Amidst the terror and destruction of the land, Isaiah boldly confesses, at God's command, that he and his children are signs and symbols to the world of the Lord's goodness and mercy. As Christian families, we are also God's witnesses to the world of Who Christ is and what He means. 1 John 4 drives this point home, encouraging followers of Jesus to be bold in abundant love to the unrighteous.

God sees every sin of every individual, both repentant and unrepentant, desiring that all come to the knowledge of the truth. He sees your children as forgiven individuals, created for a special purpose in this world. He forgives you for grouping kids together for mere convenience and often attributing to them sinful intentions rather than childish curiosities. And even if the world may choose to reject the signs and wonders of your family in its midst, He prepares you all to be witnesses to His love.

Our hearts let new-created be,
Our walk make pure and holy.
Help us offense and sin to flee,
And ever serve God solely,
So that our faith in Christ, our Lord,
May prove itself in deed and word
Before the world about us. (26:3)

For Further Reading: Isaiah 8; 1 John 4:17–21

A Refuge Reassuring

"The wolf also shall dwell with the lamb, The leopard shall lie down with the young goat, The calf and the young lion and the fatling together; And a little child shall lead them.... The nursing child shall play by the cobra's hole, And the weaned child shall put his hand in the viper's den. They shall not hurt nor destroy in all My holy mountain." Isaiah 11:6,8–9

Whether we are considering car seat options, health care professionals, or driver's ed training, the safety of our children is on the forefront of the minds of most mothers. We'd never let our kids hang out with ferocious animals, like wolves, wildcats, and snakes! But, the eternal day will come when we won't need to concern ourselves with our children's safety. Yet, even now, here on earth, God gives us a taste of safety in His refuge and strength.

When you harbor concerns about the adequacy of your parenting skills, remember both your own and your child's baptism. You have been washed in the water imbued by God with saving power. Your child has been brought to those same saving waters, washed through Jesus' death and resurrection. Together on this earth, you are both caught in a cycle of sin, but also both freed in Christ's cycle of forgiveness. You have faith, forgiveness, and new life in Christ. God can turn even parenting failures into good for His children who love Him. In both temporal and eternal concerns, take refuge in our Father's grace.

> *And when they leave their childhood home,*
> *When Satan comes alluring,*
> *May their baptismal grace become*
> *A refuge reassuring!*
> *Blest they who then can say:*
> *"God's cov'nant stands for aye."*
> *They ne'er shall be undone*
> *Who trusts in God alone—*
> *God is their mighty Father! (514:4)*

For Further Reading: Isaiah 11; Genesis 50:15–21

Mother Bird

"For You have been a strength to the poor, A strength to the needy in his distress, A refuge from the storm, A shade from the heat....You will keep him in perfect peace, Whose mind is stayed on You, Because he trusts in You." Isaiah 25:4, 26:3

If the enemy was crouching at your doorstep, what would you do? Run and hide, fearful for your life? The Assyrians are on the march toward the Promised Land, but Isaiah reminds the people with quiet confidence that God is their refuge.

There's nothing quite like motherhood to point out all of our flaws, weaknesses, and vulnerabilities. We are without strength of our own in this storm of life amidst our children, constantly on the brink of war. Even the best laid plans fail. With tears in our eyes, we cry out to God in our distress!

With all of our "mother bird" responsibilities toward our "chicks," comfort and help often seem elusive. All mothers need a little mothering themselves, and God provides just that. Psalm 91 reminds us of the peace that each Christian possesses, even through constant demands, sleepless nights, and worries galore. You can hide in the Almighty's shadow, a shadow that would one day be spread in the silhouette of a cross against the backdrop of a dark sky, as your Savior cried out in agony on your behalf. God has already rescued His "chicks" from the snare of the Hunter, the threatening Enemy. Now, every day, He covers you with His nurturing wings. God's peace is for you and your children, whatever your circumstances may be.

Other refuge have I none;
Hangs my helpless soul on Thee.
Leave, ah, leave me not alone, Still support and comfort me!
All my trust on Thee is stayed, All my help from Thee I bring;
Cover my defenseless head
With the shadow of Thy wing. (209:2)

For Further Reading: Isaiah 25; Psalm 91:1–4

Supermoms?

"Lord, you establish peace for us; all that we have accomplished you have done for us." Isaiah 26:12 (NIV)

Have you had any "supermom" moments lately? It might be something as mundane as getting all of the kids to their activities on time and coming home to a hot meal in the crock-pot. But, it sure does feel fulfilling when everything comes together! We enjoy those moments, feeling good about our vocation!

But, let's be honest. Much of the time, we don't feel like "supermom" at all. We fail, not just in getting kids someplace on time, or remembering to have a meal ready, but sometimes, also in the big things that matter: giving hugs instead of being angry, taking the time to show interest in our children's accomplishments, having devotions instead of collapsing on the couch in exhaustion after a long day. These times often over-shadow any "super-mom" moments. And yet, we can rest, even amidst our failures, knowing that anything we do wrong, or fail to do, is forgiven by God in Christ.

What a blessing it is when we feel like "super-mom," even if it isn't that often! And what a blessing to know that our success in those moments doesn't depend on our own good luck, but rather on the ability of God to use moms to bless others in their midst. Anything good we accomplish as mothers is a gift from God. We can glory in the Lord during those times, thanking and praising Him, and during all the other times, rest in His forgiving love!

In Jesus' name Our work must all be done
If it shall compass our true good and aim,
And not end in shame alone;
For ev'ry deed Which in it doth proceed,
Success and blessing gains Till it the goal attains.
Thus we honor God on high And ourselves are blessed thereby;
Wherein our true good remains. (4:1)

For Further Reading: Isaiah 26:1–16; 2 Corinthians 10:12–18

"Enjoy These Days!"

"Come, my people, enter your chambers, And shut your doors behind you; Hide yourself, as it were, for a little moment, Until the indignation is past." Isaiah 26:20

Tell me that I'm not the only one who, when reading this passage, imagines myself hiding behind the locked door of the bathroom, sheltered until my toddler's tantrum has passed? Well-meaning folks instruct moms to "enjoy these days." But "these days" can be just plain difficult. In fact, many a day, it is exceedingly easier to hide away for a moment of peace and quiet, than it is to "enjoy."

Though this application might seem vogue in modern times, the passage above is, of course, not encouraging moms to hide in their bathrooms. In it, Isaiah advises the Israelites to wait and hope in the Lord during the discipline He is sending. The terror of the enemy will only last for a time. Later, God will rescue His people and restore His kingdom.

What is the Christian's antidote to the fear and indignation of difficult days and moments? Perhaps it isn't possible to "enjoy" each and every moment with our children, but we *can* give thanks for each and every moment, each and every day, past, present, and future. We thank the Lord that the daily challenges of motherhood won't last forever as our children grow and learn. But most of all, we thank God that we, and our children, have no reason to fear spiritual punishment because of Jesus' atoning death. We hide ourselves in our daily vocations, for a little while, full of confidence that God will soon establish His eternal kingdom and bring us all to Heaven.

Thanks we give and adoration
For Thy Gospel's joyful sound.
May the fruits of Thy salvation In our hearts and lives abound.
May Thy presence, may Thy presence
With us evermore be found. (588:2)

For Further Reading: Isaiah 26:17–21; Hebrews 13:14–16

No Pow'r to Justify

"[The Israelites]...had not cleansed themselves, yet they ate the Passover contrary to what was written. But Hezekiah prayed for them, saying, 'May the good Lord provide atonement for everyone who prepares his heart to seek God...though he is not cleansed according to the purification of the sanctuary.' And the Lord listened to Hezekiah and healed the people."
2 Chronicles 30:18–20

What was God thinking?! Didn't He just spend much of the Pentateuch setting up a sacrificial system to maintain purity among Israel, and much of the prophets condemning Israel for failing to keep His laws? Why would He suddenly change His mind and allow the "unclean" to eat His covenant meal? From where does this bending of the rules come? Shouldn't He justly punish those who transgress His law?

Wait a minute! Isn't this line of thinking pretty harsh? Shouldn't we be relieved by the compassion of both Hezekiah, interceding on behalf of his people, and of God, mercifully accepting the sincere worship of His children? But then, we look at our own mothering.

Do you demand virtue from your children? Are you frustrated when they sin, instead of acknowledging that sinners do exactly that? Do you try to manipulate and control their behavior? Thank God for this Old Testament example of His mercy and grace! It isn't our righteousness that saves us. It is the mercy of the Lord that saves both our children from their imperfections, and us from our demands of their perfection.

The Law is good; but since the Fall
Its holiness condemns us all;
It dooms us for our sin to die And has no pow'r to justify.
To Jesus we for refuge flee, Who from the curse has set us free,
And humbly worship at His throne,
Saved by His grace through faith alone. (492:5,6)

For Further Reading: 2 Chronicles 30; Titus 3:4–7

Since Mortals Can No Help Afford

"Hear the words of the great king, the king of Assyria! Thus says the king: 'Do not let Hezekiah deceive you, for he will not be able to deliver you; nor let Hezekiah make you trust in the Lord.... Make peace with me by a present...and every one of you eat from his own vine and...his own fig tree, and every one of you drink the waters of his own cistern.'" Isaiah 36:13–16

The envoy of King Sennacherib called out to the leaders of Israel, dangling false and empty promises in front of them. With the threat of imminent invasion, who wouldn't want to imagine a peaceful home and prosperous land? But, the king of Assyria merely wanted to make his capture easy. He had no intent of fulfilling these promises to the Israelites, and God knew as much.

Even today, the world threatens this and pledges that, but God's promises are good and sure. What false promises of the world are tempting you today? Perhaps you wonder if you would be more content with different circumstances, more money, or fewer hindrances. If you are able to work toward positive change in your life by Godly means, certainly do so. However, if the ambitions of the world tempt you with false promises, remember Abraham, the father of the Israelites, who was convinced that God was able to perform everything He had promised. His greatest promise was fulfilled through Abraham's seed, Jesus. But God also implements His earthly promises through your motherly service to your children, His children. God will also keep His promise to uphold you during the difficult trials of your sometimes mundane, but incredibly important, vocation.

Trust not in princes, they are but mortal;
Earth-born they are and soon decay.
Naught are their counsels at life's last portal,
When the dark grave doth claim its prey.
Since mortals can no help afford,
Trust ye in Christ, our God and Lord. Alleluia, alleluia! (497:2)

For Further Reading: Isaiah 36 and 37; Romans 4:20–25

Purpose and Meaning

"For Sheol cannot thank You, Death cannot praise You;
Those who go down to the pit cannot hope for Your truth.
The living, the living man, he shall praise You, As I do this day;
The father shall make known Your truth to the children."
Isaiah 38:18–19

If you are reading this devotion right now, you must be alive. But, why are you alive? What is your purpose in life? Some mothers may easily identify purpose and meaning in their lives, but it might be a challenge for others. Some mothers have even longed for the rest that death would provide.

The passage above identifies two purposes for the living. The first is to praise the Lord. As long as we have life and breath, God intends that we praise Him in our words and actions. The second purpose is to teach our children the ways of the Lord. Living things pass away, but God's Word is forever. There are so many good and beautiful things we can become busy teaching our children about: safety, home economics, finances, world affairs. But all of this education is mere distraction if our children are not first taught God's Word. Postpone all the other good things in life to prioritize teaching your children God's unending love in Jesus, preparing them for their eternal home! And from that overflowing love, fill your home with God's praises! No matter the circumstances of your life, God has bestowed your vocation as a mother with meaning and purpose.

For as a tender father Hath pity on his children here,
[God] in His arms will gather All who are His in childlike fear.
He knows how frail our powers Who but from dust are made.
We flourish like the flowers, And even so we fade.
The wind but o'er them passes, And all their bloom is o'er—
We wither like the grasses; Our place knows us no more.
God's grace alone endureth, And children's children yet shall prove
How He with strength assureth
The hearts of all that seek His love. (456:3,4a)

For Further Reading: Isaiah 38; Isaiah 40:8

Little Lambs

"He will feed His flock like a shepherd; He will gather the lambs with His arm, And carry them in His bosom, And gently lead those who are with young." Isaiah 40:11

The first time I remember reading this Scripture passage, it was tacked to the door of a friend's refrigerator. The scrawled handwriting led me to believe it was specifically chosen to fit the occasion of this mother who was recently widowed with many young children. The impact of that verse for frightened, exhausted mothers has never left me.

There are times when motherhood feels simply overwhelming. The needs are rarely fulfilled. The tasks are never-ending. However, you are never alone in these tasks; God is doing them through you for the good of your children. Your Good Shepherd will not just lead the young, but gently lead those who are *with* young, namely, you! He carries you on His chest and comforts you when times get rough, just as you would pick up and rock a fussy child.

Motherhood is a lot like the journey of a flock climbing a rocky cliff. Looking at the present, all you can see are the impediments in your path. But looking back to the past, you have the advantage of a beautiful view, even though there may have been craggy gulches to crawl through. The trials of both the past and present may be real and difficult, but look how far God has brought you, His little lamb, and all of the little lambs in your care! And, with eagerness, look forward to the future of Heaven, to where we will someday be conveyed in Christ's capable arms.

> *I love my Shepherd's voice,*
> *His watchful eyes shall keep*
> *My wand'ring soul among*
> *The thousands of His sheep:*
> *He feeds His flock, He calls their names,*
> *His bosom bears the tender lambs. (289:4)*

For Further Reading: Isaiah 40:1–11; Psalm 23

Flying High

"The everlasting God, the Lord, The Creator of the ends of the earth, Neither faints nor is weary. His understanding is unsearchable. He gives power to the weak, And to those who have no might He increases strength. Even the youths shall faint and be weary And the young men shall utterly fall, But those who wait on the Lord Shall renew their strength; They shall mount up with wings like eagles, They shall run and not be weary, They shall walk and not faint." Isaiah 40:28–31

The lives of God's people were filled with uncertainty. Would they be invaded? Would they be taken captive to a strange and foreign land? Fear and uncertainty can be draining. Motherhood often has moments of fear and uncertainty, like when it comes to health, finances, or education.

Even if there are no major uncertainties in your life, the physical demands of motherhood itself can be exhausting: growing or nursing a baby (or both!) who depends on your body for nourishment, getting up (and staying up!) with sick children at night, trying to find a balance between one's own self-care and selfishness. We grow weary of both the uncertainties and the physical needs around us. We sometimes feel like we can't go on.

You *can* go on, however, but it isn't by mustering your own strength. It is only through the gift of God's strength. When you are falling, He comes underneath you, lifting you up and soaring like an eagle, giving you rest and refreshment for whatever tomorrow's uncertainties and physical demands may be. Don't rely on your own reserves, but trust in the Lord's providence and Christ's certain forgiveness.

Praise to the Lord, who o'er all things so wondrously reigneth,
Who, as on wings of an eagle, uplifteth, sustaineth.
Hast thou not seen
How thy desires all have been
Granted in what He ordaineth? (65:2)

For Further Reading: Isaiah 40:12–31; Hebrews 4:9–10

Drowned

*"Fear not, for I have redeemed you; I have called you by your
name; You are Mine. When you pass through the waters, I will
be with you; And through the rivers, they shall not overflow you.
When you walk through the fire, you shall not be burned,
Nor shall the flame scorch you." Isaiah 43:1–2*

The Book of Isaiah has numerous difficult passages, many of
which are filled with God's righteous indignation. But passages
like the one above, filled with incredible solace and comfort, make
reading Isaiah worth the effort.

Who hasn't felt figuratively burned, put through the flames?
Who hasn't been overwhelmed, drowning in problems and
sorrows? Yet, God does not send you alone to these trials; rather,
He sends you through them with His divine presence. When you
deserved His wrath and punishment, like the nation of Israel, only
the Holy One of Israel condescended to walk through the trials of
sinners for you.

Indeed, God has brought you out of the water, but only first
by a drowning and death. When the minister poured water on you
in the name of the Trinity, God buried you with Christ in His
grave—effecting the forgiveness of your sins, delivering you from
death and the devil, and giving eternal salvation to all who
believe. Our Heavenly Father not only walks with you in the daily
trials and burdens of motherhood, but He also sent Christ to
rescue you from the eternal punishment that your sins deserve.

> *Not fire, nor sword, nor thunder,*
> *Shall sever me from Thee;*
> *Though earth be rent asunder*
> *Thou'rt mine eternally.*
> *Not hunger, thirst, nor danger,*
> *Not pain, nor pinching want,*
> *Nor mighty princes' anger,*
> *My fearless soul shall daunt. (517:13)*

For Further Reading: Isaiah 43; Romans 6:3–4

Breasts and Hands

"Can a woman forget her nursing child, And not have compassion on the son of her womb? Surely they may forget, Yet I will not forget you. See, I have inscribed you on the palms of My hands." Isaiah 49:15–16

In this passage, God speaks to His children with all of the warmth, tenderness, and reassurance of a breastfeeding mother. Women who have nursed a baby understand that, even if distracted by a project or travel, her body will not let her forget to nurse or pump. When her breasts fill to capacity with milk, there will be physical consequences for her—an unwanted milk letdown, inflammation, or even pain and infection. But, even if a nursing mother could forget her child, God *cannot* forget His children.

Think of how often you use your hands to serve your family on a daily basis. You use them, you see them, hundreds of times a day. Christ's hands are literally inscribed with His love for you—they were ripped open in anguish with nails on the cross. The moment of His crucifixion and death was the culmination of all of the prophecies of longing and hope in the Old Testament. Jesus gave His life in your place, washing away all of your sins, giving you peace with God.

Like a mom with the names of her children tattooed on her hands, or a lactating mother, God has you constantly on His mind. He planned His rescue mission through Jesus from eternity because He loves you so much. What a beautiful picture God shows of His heart through the hands and breasts of a mother!

The Lord forsaketh not His flock,
His chosen generation;
He is their Refuge and their Rock,
Their Peace and their Salvation.
As with a mother's tender hand
He leads His own, His chosen band—
To God all praise and glory! (435:4)

For Further Reading: Isaiah 49; John 20:24–27

Beautiful Feet

"How beautiful upon the mountains Are the feet of him who brings good news, Who proclaims peace, Who brings glad tidings of good things, Who proclaims salvation, Who says to Zion, 'Your God reigns!'" Isaiah 52:7

Mothers don't often have time for all of the self-care they'd like. For instance, look at your toenails. Are they sadly in need of some pampering, painting, or a pedicure? The good news is that however calloused or lowly your feet may appear, God calls them beautiful!

Your children are a little Zion in your midst. They are God's people, bought with Christ's life-giving blood. And you are God's messenger to them, bringing them His good news. How can your child call on God if he doesn't believe? How can she believe if she hasn't heard the Gospel? How can he hear the Gospel unless someone teaches him? The apostle Paul teaches that faith comes by hearing the Word of God. Jesus says that those who hear the Word of God and keep it are blessed (Lk. 11:28). Unfortunately, we haven't always been faithful stewards of this mission; thankfully, we dwell in Christ's forgiveness for all of our failures.

What a privilege it is as a mother to read Bible stories to your children, to sit by their bedside, singing words of the faith, to pray with them and for them, to take advantage of opportunities to talk about God's law and His love! As a messenger of God's love to your children, He calls your feet beautiful! He uses you as a mother, day in and day out, to accomplish His proclamation of peace to His people.

Take my hands and let them move At the impulse of Thy love.
Take my feet and let them be
Swift and beautiful for Thee.
Take my voice and let me sing Always, only, for my King.
Take my lips and let them be
Filled with messages from Thee. (444:2,3)

For Further Reading: Isaiah 52; Nahum 1:15; Romans 10:14–17

Spiritual Fasting

"Is not [the fast that God has chosen] to share your bread with the hungry, And that you bring to your house the poor who are cast out; When you see the naked, that you cover him, And not hide yourself from your own flesh?" Isaiah 58:7

In the Pentateuch, fasting was required for the Day of Atonement. It was also often practiced in times of repentance, illness, or war. A reader might expect that God, in the middle of the Book of Isaiah, might be chastising the Israelites for not keeping the prescribed fasts. Instead, God excuses the lack of the action of fasting, focusing instead on what is more important: the condition of the heart.

Certainly, there are times when we as mothers have the wrong heart. We despise God's gift of children. We showcase a negative attitude rather than giving thanks for His daily blessings. Our Heavenly Father urges you to repent for the sin of your cold heart. He forgives you, sending you the Holy Spirit to take up permanent residence in your soul through faith in Christ!

Now, as baptized Christians, we seek to show our gratefulness to the Almighty. We needn't look far to find ways to do this, though: God declares that doing good to those in our midst is better than a fast! Mothers share their bread with the hungry at least three times a day! Mothers provide a warm and nurturing shelter for the vulnerable. Mothers buy or make clothing for bodies that continually grow. Mothers, whether they'd like to or not, cannot hide from their own flesh and blood, comforting children with attention and affection. Mothers "fast" each day, caring for their families. Viewed through the lens of Jesus' perfection, what you are doing *already* is a spiritual sacrifice with which God is well-pleased (Heb. 13:16).

> *But worthless is my sacrifice, I own it;*
> *Yet, Lord, for love's sake Thou wilt not disown it;*
> *Thou wilt accept my gift in Thy great meekness*
> *Nor shame my weakness. (292:14)*

For Further Reading: Isaiah 58; Galatians 6:9–10

Drink Deeply

*"[All who love Jerusalem] may feed and be satisfied With the
consolation of her bosom, That you may drink deeply and be
delighted With the abundance of her glory....Then you shall feed;
On her sides shall you be carried, And be dandled on her knees.
As one whom his mother comforts, So I will comfort you;
And you shall be comforted in Jerusalem." Isaiah 66:11–13*

Most moms would love to have the "problem" of an abundant milk supply! In this passage, God likens Jerusalem to a mother with bounteous milk, ready to soothe and comfort her children in all of their hardships.

Traditionally, the Holy Christian Church has been called the "mother" of believers. She is the bride of Christ, and births her children through baptism in the Holy Spirit. The Church nourishes Christians through God's Word and the Lord's Supper. She disciplines us with the preaching of the law. She comforts us with the preaching of the Gospel. She clothes us in the righteous robe of Christ. Our mother, the Church, is where our Jerusalem can fill us with abundant spiritual milk.

Even though mothers know the important benefits of the Divine Service, getting through church can be difficult. Babies and toddlers can be distracting or need guidance. Sometimes just getting everyone out the door of the house is the major challenge. Whether you are able to sit tranquilly in the pew, need to bounce a baby on your hip in the narthex, or even view the service online at a later time, drink deeply of the peace in Christ that God delivers to you in church, in His Word and Sacraments.

> *Peace to us the Church doth tell,*
> *'Tis her welcome and farewell:*
> *Peace was our baptismal dow'r,*
> *Peace shall bless our dying hour;*
> *Peace be with you, full and free,*
> *Now and through eternity. (595:2)*

For Further Reading: Isaiah 66; Ephesians 5:29–32

Afraid of the Dark

"I will wait for the God of my salvation; My God will hear me....
When I fall, I will arise; When I sit in darkness, The Lord will
be a light to me. I will bear the indignation of the Lord,
Because I have sinned against Him, Until He pleads my case
And executes justice for me. He will bring me forth to the light;
I will see His righteousness." Micah 7:7–9

While Isaiah foretold the coming of Assyria against Judah, the prophet Micah foretold the fall of Samaria, the Northern Kingdom's capital. You might recognize the words of Micah from the passage recited at children's Christmas programs: "But you, Bethlehem Ephrathah..." (5:2) or from Christian T-shirts and posters: "Do justly, love mercy, walk humbly" (6:8).

Just as a child having a nightmare screams and calls for "Mommy," this book beautifully pictures a believer waiting on the Lord amid judgment, darkness. She trusts that God will execute justice on her behalf, even though she may not understand how this will work. The believer doesn't hope in her own "good" deeds to bring light to the situation, finding only dark failure in them.

Rather than punish you for your sins, God chose to execute justice in a different way. Jesus speaks words of comfort to you: "I AM the light of the world." God gives you light, hope, and comfort by laying your dark deeds on Jesus. His full and free exchange on the cross brings calm to the nightmare of our troubling sins. His sweet salvation extends to your whole family and knits hearts together in love, even when fearful of the dark.

> *When Jesus enters meek and lowly*
> *To fill the home with sweetest peace;*
> *When hearts have felt His blessing holy*
> *And found from sin complete release;*
> *Then light and calm within shall reign*
> *And hearts divided love again. (111:2)*

For Further Reading: The Book of Micah; John 8:12

Secrets, Secrets

"Also the children of Israel secretly did against the Lord their God things that were not right, and they built for themselves high places in all their cities, from watchtower to fortified city."
2 Kings 17:9

Have you ever stumbled upon your child, Sharpie in hand, making a secret masterpiece on the furniture? From rather harmless secrets that little ones hope to keep, to the larger, consequential secrets that tweens and teens try to keep, no family is immune from secrets. But, children aren't the only ones with secrets. As parents, we have secrets of our own. Many of us have mothering habits we'd never admit to. We'd be ashamed if our peers knew that we shouted so often, cleaned the toilet so little, or harbored so much resentment. The Israelites of the Northern Kingdom had their "secret," too: idolatry, and because of it, God allowed the Assyrians to carry them off into slavery, in order to bring about repentance.

Secrets are never truly hidden from God (Ps. 139:1). He knows we have strayed from His ways like lost sheep and followed the devices and desires of our hearts. He knows we have offended against His holy law. He knows we have done those things which we should not have done, and not done those things which we should have done. Our innermost thoughts, words, and deeds are made bare before Him. God had a secret (Mt. 13:35), but He has no need to keep it any longer: He planned from eternity to save you from your wickedness and depravity. The fall into sin by our first parents has been remedied by Christ, and revealed through Him. No more secrets needed.

Thy work alone, O Christ, Can ease this weight of sin;
Thy blood alone, O Lamb of God, Can give me peace within.
Thy love to me, O God, Not mine, O Lord to Thee,
Can rid me of this dark unrest And set my spirit free. (433:2)

For Further Reading: 2 Kings 17; Deuteronomy 29:29

Like Mother, Like Child

"So [the formerly heathen nations who had been transplanted into Samaria] feared the Lord, yet served their carved images; also their children and their children's children have continued doing as their fathers did, even to this day." 2 Kings 17:41

It's no surprise that children pattern themselves after the adults to whom they are closest. Some of the most amusing play for toddlers has nothing to do with toys; they simply imitate their parents—trying to cook, clean, and even work on the computer! In fact, years ago at a visit to the pediatrician, our doctor noted that my daughter's vocal inflection exactly matched my own.

Unfortunately, this universal habit means that our children also mimic our shortfalls and wickedness. If a son hears a mother swear, he'll use that word before long. If a daughter witnesses a father's ritual overeating, she'll think it perfectly normal. If children recognize the lack of passion their parents have for God's Word, they may be apt to push aside their own zeal.

Praise the Lord that Jesus was once a child, too, who patterned His own life after the love and mercy of His Father. Jesus' childhood, adolescence, and adulthood, along with His passion, death, and resurrection, broke the vicious cycle of both inherited and learned sin. As God's children through baptism, we take comfort in His perfection given to us despite all of our personal shortcomings.

Giv'n from on high to me;
I cannot rise to Thee.
O cheer my wearied spirit:
O pure and holy Child,
Through all Thy grace and merit,
Blest Jesus, Lord most mild,
Draw me unto Thee!
Draw me unto Thee! (135:2)

For Further Reading: 2 Kings 17; 2 Timothy 3:15

The Solid Rock

*"The Lord is good, A stronghold in the day of trouble;
And He knows those who trust in Him. But with an overflowing
flood He will make an utter end of [Nineveh],
And darkness will pursue His enemies." Nahum 1:7–8*

Most of the 12 minor prophets give judgments and consolation to God's people, but by contrast, Nahum prophesied against the heathen city of Nineveh. Decades earlier, this capital city of Assyria was shown God's mercy by the reluctant Jonah. As a society, they repented of their sins, but only temporarily. God later used the Babylonians to destroy the Ninevites, so much so that their city was never again rebuilt. The name "Nahum" means "comfort." This short passage from the book bearing his name certainly does just that for those whose hope is in the Lord.

A stronghold, a rock, a stay, a fortress. The Bible, hymns, and the liturgy use these names to represent the protection of God. Whatever "castle-like" word is used, above all, the Lord is good. Under His kingly protection, His subjects remain secure, and under His wrath, all enemies flee to their destruction.

What mother doesn't find comfort knowing that she's under God's protection? God certainly knows all of our earthly enemies: finances, discipline, health concerns, worries. He brandishes His sword against them. But even more, He intimately knows our spiritual enemies: Satan, the world, and our own sinful flesh, overwhelming them in the flood of His own blood. When our failures confront us, washing away any earthly foundation we had hoped to establish for our loved ones, Christ washes away our sins, wraps us in His royal forgiveness and love, and secures us on solid ground.

> *His oath, His covenant, and blood
> Support me in the whelming flood;
> When ev'ry earthly prop gives way,
> He then is all my Hope and Stay.
> On Christ, the solid Rock, I stand;
> All other ground is sinking sand. (197:3)*

For Further Reading: The Book of Nahum; Psalm 100:5

Quiet Souls

"Sing, O daughter of Zion!...Be glad and rejoice with all your heart, O daughter of Jerusalem!...The Lord your God in your midst, The Mighty One, will save; He will quiet you with His love, He will rejoice over you with singing." Zephaniah 3:14,17

Zephaniah served the Lord with his three chapters of prophecy during the reign of King Josiah. The prophet was a great-great-grandson of King Hezekiah. In our vocation as mothers, it's easy to forget that we, too, are daughters, royal heirs, not to an earthly king, but to the Most High God!

And yet, even with the kingdom at our fingertips, under the loving, caring control of our Father, we often find ourselves discontent, with souls moaning dissonant chords. We look around and find ourselves jealous of other women's skills, circumstances, and lives, even though we are God's royal daughters. Our sinful hearts are disquiet, yearning for the cacophony of the pleasures and pursuits outside the safe boundaries established by our benevolent King.

However, the King sings over you harmoniously with His Word and Sacraments, quieting your longings, reuniting you to Himself and His will through Christ! Commanded by our Lord to sing and rejoice, we find the strength to do so given by the power of the Holy Spirit. Even through our personal struggles against discontent, we ultimately look forward to a perfectly fulfilled, quiet satisfaction: singing God's eternal praises in Heaven.

Why art thou disquiet within me?
Why art thou cast down, O my soul?
Confide in thy God, let Him win thee!
Still hope in thy God, Him extol!
For surely once dawneth a morrow,
When, freed from thy care and thy sorrow,
Thou praises shalt sing to thy God. (462:6)

For Further Reading: The Book of Zephaniah; Psalm 42

Jeremiah, and You

"'Before I formed you in the womb I knew you; Before you were born I sanctified you; I ordained you a prophet to the nations.' Then said I: 'Ah, Lord God! Behold, I cannot speak, for I am a youth.' But the Lord said to me: 'Do not say, "I am a youth," For you shall go to all to whom I send you, And whatever I command you, you shall speak.'" Jeremiah 1:5–7

Jeremiah is the longest book of the Bible and its length spans several decades, from King Josiah's reign through the Babylonian Captivity. The book intimately shows us the personal struggles of the man, the prophet. Jeremiah was commanded not to marry or have children because of the tumultuous times. He is also known as the "weeping prophet" due to his vivid descriptions of grief regarding his beloved people and country.

While the verses above were given by God specifically for His servant Jeremiah, they ring true for us as well. God knows you. He planned for your birth, childhood, marriage, and parenting. He also knows that you have failed in those vocations, polluting yourself, and yet He loves you so much that He washed you clean in Christ's blood. He has given you His Word and the Holy Spirit to share His love with others, just as He did for Jeremiah.

Like Jeremiah, neither youth nor inability disqualify the called for God's service. Did God make you a mother when you were young? Perhaps your children are young? Or, like many mothers, maybe you feel inexperienced, doubtful of your ability when it comes to raising children? In any case, God has been with you since before you could even remember, and He remains with you today, equipping you to serve Him and His children.

Father, Son, and Holy Ghost, Bless the young before Thee;
Thou their wants and dangers know'st
Watch then, we implore Thee.
Here they stand, Hopeful band,
Faith in Thee confessing, Waiting for Thy blessing. (509:1)

For Further Reading: Jeremiah 1; 1 Timothy 4:12–13

A Future and a Hope

"For thus says the Lord: After seventy years are completed at Babylon, I will visit you and perform My good word toward you, and cause you to return to this place. For I know the thoughts that I think toward you, says the Lord, thoughts of peace and not of evil, to give you a future and a hope. Then you will call upon Me and go and pray to Me, and I will listen to you. And you will seek Me and find Me, when you search for Me with all your heart." Jeremiah 29:10–13

The comforting words above were sent by God through Jeremiah to the Israelite captives who had now been transported to Babylon, as foretold by so many of the previous prophets. Even though the Israelites may have had a limited view of success, perceiving God's future vengeance on Babylon and Edom as the ultimate goal (see Psalm 137), they hoped for return to Jerusalem, trusting in God's promises through hopeless times.

The modern blessings of home and family have little comparison to slavery in a foreign land, and yet, our lives can still be filled with fear and grief, heavy with longing for something "different." Your earthly life may not look like success to the world, just as the Babylonian captives looked defeated. And yet, God promises you a future and a hope, as He did His Old Testament followers. Because of Jesus' death and resurrection, God will someday transport you from this valley of sorrow to Himself in Heaven. Even though you struggle on earth with every evil of body and soul, what an amazing future and hope await you!

Grant us, dear Lord, some vision brief
Of future triumph telling,
Gilding with hope our night of grief,
Our clouds of fear dispelling.
If the dim foretaste was so bright,
O what shall be the dazzling light
Of Thine eternal dwelling! (225:3)

For Further Reading: Jeremiah 29; Isaiah 65:17–25

The Sacrifice

"The iniquity of Israel shall be sought, but there shall be none;
And the sins of Judah, but they shall not be found;
For I will pardon those whom I preserve." Jeremiah 50:20

"Time-out" is a common discipline technique when a child spends some quiet time thinking about his or her misbehavior. When the appointed time is over, the parent and child conference about the infraction. In a way, the Babylonian Captivity was a figurative "time-out" for God's people...except during the Parent-child conference, no wrongdoing could be found!

God just spent a good portion of the Old Testament accusing the Israelites of their sins, making list after list of their iniquities! But now, no sins can be found? How can this be? Was it somehow because of the system of animal sacrifices? No, God's people weren't keeping the sacrifices anyway, and even when they did, it was with sin-filled hearts. Those sacrifices were, even at their best, but a shadow of the Sacrifice to come.

The Israelites were sent to Babylon; we deserve an eternal "time-out" in Hell. Think of all the ways you sin daily in your vocation as mother: Neglect, worry, apathy, anger. No amount of personal resolution or sacrifice can remove those sins from your record. Only God can. The ultimate fulfillment of the Old Testament sacrificial system was found in Jesus. He gave His life once, for all. God doesn't just momentarily put aside our sins, ready to trot them out later for revenge! Instead, He has paid the full price for our wickedness and rebellion: the blood of His Son.

The same enduring forgiveness that Israel experienced is yours. You are dear to God. You have been washed of your mothering foibles and failures in Jesus, pardoned and preserved.

> *Where'er the greatest sins abound, By grace they are exceeded;*
> *Thy helping hand is always found With aid where aid is needed.*
> *Our Shepherd good and true is He Who will at last His Israel free*
> *From all their sin and sorrow. (452:5)*

For Further Reading: Jeremiah 50; Hebrews 10:11–18

His Compassions Fail Not

"My soul still remembers [my affliction] And sinks within me. This I recall to my mind, Therefore I have hope. Through the Lord's mercies we are not consumed, Because His compassions fail not. They are new every morning; Great is Your faithfulness. It is good that one should hope and wait quietly For the salvation of the Lord." Lamentations 3:20–23,26

The Book of Lamentations is thought to have been authored by Jeremiah, expressing his profound agony at the plight of the Hebrews. There's hardly a positive phrase in the entire five chapters, except for the passage above. Sandwiched in the middle of the book of poetry, the center of chapter three offers a bright light of hope to Israel during a season of desolation.

As mothers, we also have desolate seasons. We have desperate days, and weeks, and months. And for those despondent times when we aren't the mothers we ought to be, we cling to God's faithful forgiveness in Christ. When you arise to start a new day, you have the sure hope that God's compassions fail not and His mercies are new every morning! Because you are a baptized child of God, rest assured that He will display the same compassion and mercy in your life as He did throughout the lives of the Old Testament characters: Job, Abraham, Jacob, Joseph, Moses, Joshua, Gideon, Ruth, Hannah, Samuel, David, Solomon, and the Prophets.

And so, we hope and we wait. Jeremiah and the Jews awaited the end of the Babylonian Captivity in the short-term, and they awaited the appearance of the Messiah in the long-term. Modern-day Christians look back to Jesus' sacrifice on the cross, and look forward to Christ's second coming, when all will be made right.

And though it tarry till the night And till the morning waken, My heart shall never doubt His might Nor count itself forsaken. Do thus, O ye of Israel's seed, Ye of the Spirit born indeed; Wait for your God's appearing. (452:4)

For Further Reading: Lamentations 3; James 5:11

And There Shall Be Holiness

*"For the day of the Lord upon all the nations is near; As you
have done, it shall be done to you; Your reprisal shall return
upon your own head....But on Mount Zion there shall be
deliverance, And there shall be holiness; The house of Jacob
shall possess their possessions." Obadiah 15, 17*

The Book of Obadiah is the shortest in the Old Testament,
consisting of only verses, no chapters! This prophecy was given
against the Edomites, descendants of Esau, Jacob's brother. How
heart-breaking that the children of Jacob, known as Israelites,
would be so persecuted by their blood relatives.

Sometimes, we have bullies in our own homes, too. When
encouraging their children to be kind to others, parents often
moralize, "Do unto others as you would have them do unto you."
But in the passage above, God flips the "Golden Rule" on its head
—as Edom had done evil to Judah, so evil would be done to Edom.
No transgression of the law can go unpunished.

But in His next breath, God reminds readers of His
protection over His precious remnant. In Jerusalem, on Golgatha,
Israel's final triumph would take place: atonement through the
Messiah, our holiness through Christ's sacrifice.

When you and your children have not "done to others" as you
would have them do to you, even when you or your children have
been bullies to your own blood relatives, confess your sins, be
certain of forgiveness, and dwell with God's protected remnant.

*Lamb of God, pure and holy,
Who on the cross didst suffer,
Ever patient and lowly,
Thyself to scorn didst offer.
All sins Thou borest for us,
Else had despair reigned o'er us:
Thy peace be with us, O Jesus! O, Jesus! (41:3)*

For Further Reading: The Book of Obadiah; Psalm 65:1–4

To Thee at All Times Cleave

"Though the fig tree may not blossom, Nor fruit be on the vines; Though the labor of the olive may fail, And the fields yield no food; Though the flock may be cut off from the fold, And there be no herd in the stalls—Yet I will rejoice in the Lord, I will joy in the God of my salvation." Habakkuk 3:17–18

The prophet Habakkuk may have been among the Judean exiles in 597 BC. His writings, scripted as a conversation between God and the prophet, were composed to comfort God's people and encourage them to await the Lord's goodness and timing, even when it seemed illogical. The book begins by describing the words as an "oracle," which can also be translated as "burden." Habakkuk had the vocation of carrying the difficult burden of comforting a people whose hope was nearly destroyed. The verses above come right after an elaborate review of God's providence throughout Israel's history; regardless of the circumstances of God's people, including suffering and loss, God is in control and His plan is a good plan, which ends in peace and forgiveness through Jesus. He enables us to give thanks in all circumstances.

I would venture to guess none of us has a fig tree or grape vine, but the picturesque language of Habakkuk is clear nonetheless. How might you "translate" this verse into your own life? "Though my birth plan may not be carried out, and the plumbing and heating are on the fritz; Though the food is sparse and payday is not until next week; Though I doubt my mothering choices, and sometimes feel lonely; Though the toddler is tantruming, and the teenager is rebelling; Though the laundry and dishes will never be finished—Yet I will rejoice in the Lord, I will joy in the God of my salvation."

Lord, how shall I thank Thee rightly? I acknowledge that by Thee I am saved eternally. Let me not forget it lightly But to Thee at all times cleave, And my heart true peace receive. Joy, O joy, beyond all gladness, Christ hath done away with sadness! Hence, all sorrow and repining, For the Sun of Grace is shining! (163:3)

For Further Reading: The Book of Habakkuk; Isaiah 12:3

"Speak My Words"

"You shall speak My words to them, whether they hear or whether they refuse, for they are rebellious." Ezekiel 2:7

The contents of the Book of Ezekiel take place both before and after the destruction of Jerusalem and the Temple. Ezekiel's message is similar to other prophets, but specifically focuses on the *holy*—God's holy people, the Holy Temple, and the Holy Land. Over 65 times in the book, God states, "They will know that I am the Lord." Ezekiel was witness to God's presence exiting the temple, and yet, God was never limited to any one place. He is free to judge, and He is free to be gracious and forgiving.

Three times in two chapters, God speaks the words "whether they hear or whether they refuse" to Ezekiel, commanding him to declare God's truth. Like many of the prophets, Ezekiel was sent to a people who did not accept God's message. The same can be true for mothers. Often, our children don't want to sit for devotions. They don't want to be confronted about their sins. They don't want spiritual advice. But, because God has equipped us with the truth of His Word, we continue to teach and mold, even when we don't see improvement. In fact, the Holy Spirit perseveres in the same manner with you: breaking down your stubborn heart, reminding you of God's forgiving love, and building up your faith through His Word and the Sacraments.

Even when it is a struggle, don't give up teaching your children God's Word, right and wrong, and forgiveness for their failings in Christ. God is good. Follow His commands, entrusting your children, rebellious or submissive, to the care of the Holy Spirit.

> *In these last days of sore distress*
> *Grant us, dear Lord, true steadfastness*
> *That pure we keep, till life is spent,*
> *Thy holy Word and Sacrament. (511:2)*

For Further Reading: Ezekiel 2; Isaiah 46:12–13

All Coldness from My Heart Remove

"And [the exiles] will go [back to Israel], and they will take away all its detestable things and all its abominations from there. Then I will give them one heart, and I will put a new spirit within them, and take the stony heart out of their flesh, and give them a heart of flesh." Ezekiel 11:18–19

With so much packed into our family schedules and piled onto our mothering plates, it's easy to get caught up in the desire to "get things done." How quick we are to take for granted the feelings and needs of our children, who often hunger for more tenderness and time than we are willing to give. Often, children seem like distractions from our "to-do" list and the enemy of the productivity we so desperately yearn for. A beautiful quotation, often attributed to C. S. Lewis, summarizes the positive of this sentiment simply, "Children are not a distraction from more important work, they are the most important work."

When the Lord returned His people to the Promised Land, He pledged to "trade hearts" with them, taking away their formerly hard, stony hearts, and freely giving them hearts of flesh: sensing, worshiping, and imaging God. It isn't the people who deserve or decide this, but rather God, as the Keeper of the covenant, Who generously gives this gift. Through redemption in His Son, our Father has also taken away the stony heart you often have toward your children, instead giving you a life-filled heart, full of compassion and empathy.

Oh, grant that nothing in my soul
May dwell but Thy pure love alone!
O, may Thy love possess me whole,
My Joy, my Treasure, and my Crown!
All coldness from my heart remove;
My ev'ry act, word, thought, be love. (372:2)

For Further Reading: Ezekiel 11; Jeremiah 32:37–44

Children of Abraham, Friends of God

"The soul who sins shall die. The son shall not bear the guilt of the father, nor the father bear the guilt of the son. The righteousness of the righteous shall be upon himself, and the wickedness of the wicked shall be upon himself." Ezekiel 18:20

In the passage above, God reminds His people that each of them is responsible for his own sins; no one can bank on the righteousness of another; alternatively, no one can blame someone in their ancestry for depriving them of righteousness. This passage offers little hope and no Gospel. We're all sinners, responsible for our own misdeeds. However, in the larger context of the Old Testament, there is comfort: God had a rescue mission in mind for even the gravest of sinners. From Adam to Abraham and beyond, He promises, "I will forgive their iniquity, and their sin I will remember no more" (Jer. 31:34).

This passage also gives hope that a chain of inherited habits can be broken. Perhaps you harbor trauma from your childhood experiences, desperately trying to parent differently than you were parented. Or perhaps you fear for your own children, who all too often mimic the sins they observe in you daily. Whatever evils existed in your family of origin, or alternatively, whatever evils exist in your own home, you and your children are independent of others' sins that may surround you. You personally have been made part of Abraham's family, not by birth, but by rebirth: baptism and faith in Jesus and His blood spilled for you. Regardless of your parentage or parenting, like Abraham, you are now God's friend through faith (Jas. 2:23).

The God of Abr'am praise,
Whose all-sufficient grace
Shall guide me all my pilgrim days In all my ways.
He deigns to call me friend;
He calls Himself my God.
And He shall save me to the end Through Jesus' blood. (69:3)

For Further Reading: Ezekiel 18; Romans 4:1–4

"That's Not Fair!"

"Yet you say, 'The way of the Lord is not fair.' Hear now, O house of Israel, is it not My way which is fair, and your ways which are not fair?...Yet the children of your people say, 'The way of the Lord is not fair.' But it is their way which is not fair!"
Ezekiel 18:25, 33:17

Kids like to play the part of "equality police," manipulating a difference in treatment between siblings into a perceived injustice. But often age, ability, maturity, health conditions, and a myriad of other factors determine the privileges and gifts our various offspring receive. Sometimes as parents, we actually *do* have good and just reasons for treating our children differently from others, even though it may look "unfair." Our Father has also chosen to treat His children unfairly, but it's never due to any merit or worthiness on our part! Not because of justice, always because of mercy, His unfair treatment is perpetually benevolent!

Just as our parental viewpoint about justice and equality may play out differently than our children's notions, so God's prerogative regarding "unfairness" is different from the opinion of mere humans. God has not punished you according to what your sins deserve. As Luther explains in the Second Article, your Lord "has redeemed [you], a lost and condemned creature, purchased and won [you] from all sins, from death and from the power of the devil; not with gold or silver, but with His holy, precious blood, and with His innocent suffering and death." He endured the cross and gave you His crown, to heal your soul. Thank and praise God that He *doesn't* treat you fairly.

> The load Thou takest on Thee,
> That pressed so sorely on me,
> It crushed me to the ground.
> The cross for me enduring,
> The crown for me securing,
> My healing in Thy wounds is found. (304:6)

For Further Reading: Psalm 103; Job 11:6

Turn, Turn!

"Say to them: 'As I live,' says the Lord God, 'I have no pleasure in the death of the wicked, but that the wicked turn from his way and live. Turn, turn from your evil ways! For why should you die, O house of Israel?'" Ezekiel 33:11

It would be unreasonable to think that the only reason a mother would demand that a child hold her hand while crossing the street is because she is cruel. As mature adults, we understand that rules are given for our own safety and security. In the passage above, God begs His people, in love, to turn from their wicked ways, back to His law. Today, too, He wishes life for His children, not death! Though we turn and turn and try and try to please God, we find ourselves continually returning to our deadly and wicked sins, like a child insisting on running into a busy street. It's no use to look to ourselves. Instead, the answer to our sin problem is to look to Jesus, who kept God's demands perfectly in our place.

Yet, the commands of the Lord have value. In the Old Testament, God gave His people many rules for their safety and security. While New Testament believers are no longer bound by sacrificial or governmental laws, the moral law continues to serve as a curb (controlling wild outbursts of sin), mirror (reflecting our sin), and guide (instructing Christians in God-pleasing living). The Messiah has come, keeping the law perfectly, submitting to death, and rising to life—all for you! He is also your perfect guide to sanctified living, demonstrating during His life on earth how to compassionately care for the weak, different, hurting, and confused. He empowers you to follow in His footsteps, turning from your evil inclinations to a vocation of service to the least of these in your midst.

Be Thou my Counselor, My Pattern and my Guide;
And through this desert land Still keep me by Thy side.
O let my feet ne'er run astray,
Nor rove, nor seek the crooked way. (289:3)

For Further Reading: Ezekiel 33; 1 Timothy 1:5–11

But, If Not

"Our God whom we serve is able to deliver us from the burning
fiery furnace, and He will deliver us from your hand, O king.
But if not, let it be known to you, O king, that we
do not serve your gods." Daniel 3:17–18

Daniel and his three Hebrew friends had been among the early exiles taken to Babylon, groomed for service to the king. The Book of Daniel is part narrative and part prophecy. In chapter three, the friends find themselves practicing civil disobedience—going against the government when it orders actions against God. In this case, Daniel's friends refused to worship a statue when commanded by Nebuchadnezzar. Ironically, the Israelite people as a whole experienced captivity because of their former idolatry. Now, the three men refuse to submit to the practice that got their people in trouble in the first place, reserving their worship for the Most High God.

At the time, those three men didn't have a clear picture of the outcome of their situation. Yet, they knew the character of God—His miracles in the lives of their ancestors and His faithfulness. They trusted that God *could* save them from the fiery furnace, but if not, they admitted they might not fully grasp His will—perhaps God's purpose for them included a refining fire.

We, too, admit that we don't fully understand what God's will may be for us and our children as we struggle through this life. Yet, you know God's character—His strength and faithfulness. You trust that God *could* save you from your difficulties, but if not, you know that the fiery furnace of Hell was already quenched at Jesus' cross. Your greatest need has been fulfilled, and Christ promises to be with you through any earthly refining fire.

Now I will cling forever To Christ, my Savior true;
My Lord will leave me never, Whate'er He passeth through.
He rends death's iron chain; He breaks through sin and pain;
He shatters hell's dark thrall; I follow Him through all. (341:6)

For Further Reading: The Book of Daniel; Psalm 140

For Such a Time As This

*"[Esther's cousin Mordecai said,] 'For if you remain completely
silent at this time, relief and deliverance will arise for the Jews
from another place, but you and your father's house will perish.
Yet who knows whether you have come to the kingdom
for such a time as this?'" Esther 4:14*

The Book of Esther records the history behind the Jewish festival of Purim. It stands out as unique among other books because of its complete absence of the name of God or prayer. However, the omission may have been a literary technique, used by the author to actually heighten the reader's awareness of God's assumed activity behind every event in the story. There are no mighty miracles displayed in Esther's life, but rather, the quiet power of God is demonstrated through the actions of individuals. Whether or not Esther was always conscious of God working through her to save the Jews from annihilation, she was His instrument nonetheless.

Mothers are also God's instruments in their families. Luther's explanations to the Second and Third Petitions explain that "the kingdom of God comes when...we believe His holy Word and live godly lives...[and] God's will is done when He...strengthens and keeps us steadfast in His Word and in faith until our end." God has chosen you for such a time as this, for such a child as this, and He works through you to be a blessing to your family, whether or not you are conscious of it. He uses you to share His Word, and the Savior, with His children. God doesn't *need* people to accomplish His plans, but what a blessing that He chooses us! We pray that His kingdom come and will may be done among us also.

*Thy kingdom come, Thy will be done In earth, as 'tis in heaven.
Keep us in life, by grace led on, Forgiving and forgiven;
Save Thou us in temptation's hour,
And from all ills; Thine is the pow'r,
And all the glory, Amen! (227:14)*

For Further Reading: Esther 4; 1 Corinthians 3:9–11

Sleepless Nights

"That night the king could not sleep. So one was commanded to bring the book of the records of the chronicles; and they were read before the king. And it was found written that Mordecai had told of...the doorkeepers who had sought to lay hands on [the] King." Esther 6:1–2

When the Book of Esther is read aloud during the Feast of Purim, little children are taught to hiss whenever they hear the name of Haman! Haman is the "bad guy" in the story of Esther, but also the right-hand man of Esther's husband, the king. The night before Haman plans to kill Mordecai in preparation for the obliteration of the Jewish race, God interjects. The king cannot sleep and he has his records read aloud to him. He finds that Mordecai had essentially saved the king's life, but had never been recognized for it. The next day, the king commands that Haman show honor to Mordecai, his sworn enemy, on the king's behalf.

Of course, there's more to this account than just a case of insomnia. God is working to preserve His chosen people. Nonetheless, God can and does work through sleepless nights. You might be in the baby stage, awake with a hungry newborn. Perhaps you're not sleeping because you are up caring for a sick child. Maybe you haven't yet allowed yourself the luxury of going to bed, waiting for a teenager to return home late at night. Perhaps your sleeplessness is only a stage, or perhaps your own special needs or the needs of another will make sleepless nights your new normal. In any case, instead of getting frustrated while you're awake, you can give thanks for your family members who are sleeping, remembering that your Savior dwells with you. He never slumbers nor sleeps. Pray and meditate upon His eternal love in Christ for you and your family.

My loved ones, rest securely, For God this night will surely
From peril guard your heads. Sweet slumbers may He send you
And bid His hosts attend you
And through the night watch o'er your beds. (569:6)

For Further Reading: Esther 6; Psalm 121:1–4

Time, Talents, Treasures

"Consider your ways! Go up to the mountains and bring wood and build the temple, that I may take pleasure in it and be glorified....My house...is in ruins, while every one of you runs to his own house." Haggai 1:7–9

The books of Haggai and Zechariah both encourage the exiles to return to Jerusalem and rebuild, after being given permission from Cyrus the Great, God's chosen instrument. Haggai specifically urged the remnant to restore God's temple, under Ezra's leadership.

God desires that we use our time, talent, and treasure to serve Him and bless the Church. We desire to do this because we fear and love God, hold His Word sacred, and gladly hear and learn it. We ought to teach our children to honor God and bless their congregations in the same way. While raising children is certainly God-pleasing, it also draws from the reserves of our time, talents, and treasures, allowing selfishness to creep in with excuses that we are "too" busy, "too" unpracticed, and "too" budget-conscious to be generous to God. Yes, with a prayerful and discerning heart, there are definitely appropriate seasons for saying "no" to volunteering or giving, but all too often, we justify our own greed.

But, Christ used His time to serve the needy. He used His talents, His divine power, to bless those in His midst. He used His treasure, His life to the point of death, to redeem sinners. All of this Christ has done to serve the Church: you! Having believed on His name, you are the temple of the Holy Spirit, cleansed to serve the Lord, His House, and the little children who worship there.

> *I pray Thee, dear Lord Jesus,*
> *My heart to keep and train That I Thy holy temple*
> *From youth to age remain.*
> *Turn Thou my thoughts forever*
> *From worldly wisdom's lore; If I but learn to know Thee,*
> *I shall not want for more. (178)*

For Further Reading: The Book of Haggai; 2 Corinthians 6:16

Beautiful Holiness

"The Lord their God will save them in that day,
As the flock of His people. For they shall be like the jewels
of a crown, Lifted like a banner over His land—For how great
is its goodness And how great its beauty!" Zechariah 9:16–17

The prophet Zechariah encouraged the Jews who had returned to Jerusalem to rebuild the wall for protection, under the leadership of Nehemiah. Perhaps his most well-known prophecy is that regarding Jesus on Palm Sunday, "Rejoice greatly, O daughter of Zion! Shout, O daughter of Jerusalem! Behold, your King is coming to you; He is just and having salvation, Lowly and riding on a donkey, A colt, the foal of a donkey" (9:9). In the lesser-known passage above, Zechariah speaks of God's action of saving His people. After all of their rebellion, God renews His covenant, calling His people beautiful, precious like jewels.

While most mothers would love to have their appearance compared to the jewels of a crown, we usually don't have time to fuss about our looks. We're lucky to leave the house in matching clothes, free from drool or kitchen stains! Even if your outside happens to be impeccable, how about that inside, that heart?

In the books of the Chronicles and Psalms, holiness is equated with beauty. You could sport the trendiest clothing and the most flattering hairstyle, and still be repulsive because of the inward stain of your sins, sins of vanity about your looks, dissatisfaction with your physical appearance, or covetousness for different clothing and accessories which would only improve your style and not your inner shame. And yet, God sent Jesus to renew His everlasting covenant with you. Through Jesus' blood, you have been made beautiful in His holiness, a shining and brilliant jewel. Putting on Christ's robe of righteousness, you are lovely, and as God's child, you will remain dazzling through eternity!

I am trusting Thee for cleansing In the crimson flood,
Trusting Thee to make me holy By Thy blood. (206:3)

For Further Reading: The Book of Zechariah; Isaiah 61:10

Israel's Guardian

"We...humble[d] ourselves before our God, to seek from Him the right way for us and our little ones and all our possessions.... So we fasted and entreated our God for this, and He answered our prayer....And the hand of our God was upon us, and He delivered us from the hand of the enemy and from ambush along the road. So we came to Jerusalem." Ezra 8:21,23,31–32

The books of Ezra and Nehemiah pick up Israel's history where 2 Chronicles leaves off. While the rebuilding of the temple is the main plot in Ezra, all of these smaller books of the Bible are essentially part of a larger story which unfolds God's plan of redemption. As a whole, the Old Testament is a tapestry, weaving together history, wisdom, song, and prophecy, ultimately finding fulfillment with the birth of Jesus in the manger and the death of Christ on the cross. The One Who shapes history doesn't record history for its own sake, but rather that we would marvel at His faithfulness to His promises and His grace to the undeserving.

Ezra and many Jewish families traveled across the wilderness from Babylon to Jerusalem, fulfilling God's promise to bring His people home. God is also setting the stage for the birth of the Savior to be in accord with prophecies. Besides all of the precious souls in Ezra's care, he had also been entrusted with millions of dollars worth of treasures, given by the Babylonians, to be used for rebuilding. The same God guarding Israel watches over you and your children, directing and defending you from evil. God's hand is upon you, watching and guiding your footsteps each day, washing you clean in Christ's blood, and ultimately bringing you safely to your Heavenly Jerusalem.

> *O Israel's Guardian, hear me, Watch over me this day;*
> *In all I do be near me, For others, too, I pray;*
> *To Thee I would commend them,*
> *Our Church, our school, our land,*
> *Direct them and defend them, When dangers are at hand. (86:2)*

For Further Reading: The Book of Ezra; 2 Thessalonians 3:3

Abide With Me!

"For I am the Lord, I do not change; Therefore you are not consumed, O sons of Jacob." Malachi 3:6

Just when you feel like you might have possibly figured out this mothering thing, something changes: teething, growth-spurts, milestones, diagnoses, friends, puberty, and the list goes on! Whether or not you're in the mothering groove, change can be hard! We as moms change, too. Sometimes those changes are due to the wisdom that growth and experience bring to our choices. But we also sometimes change unpredictably; we're not always consistent. We bend the rules to our own benefit. We change our minds. We swing our moods. No wonder our poor children sometimes have a hard time figuring us out!

But our Father in Heaven does not change. "Jesus Christ is the same yesterday, today, and forever" (Heb. 13:8). Because God keeps all of His promises, none of His children will be lost or destroyed. His forgiving love is constant, found first for many of us in the regenerative waters of baptism, and delivered with His body and blood in the bread and wine at the Lord's Table. Luther's Second Article states that God gives you these gifts "in order that [you] might be His own, live under Him in His kingdom, and serve Him in everlasting righteousness, innocence and blessedness; even as He is risen from the dead, lives and reigns to all eternity." These rich and unchanging promises are for you, and for your children, just as they were first made to Jacob and his children. As we come to the end of the Old Testament, we look forward with hope to the advent of the Savior, where God will clearly display His constant love in a lowly manger, on a bloody cross, and in an empty tomb: all for you! Christ, come quickly!

> *Swift to its close ebbs out life's little day;*
> *Earth's joys grow dim, its glories pass away.*
> *Change and decay in all around I see;*
> *O Thou who changest not, abide with me! (561:2)*

For Further Reading: The Book of Malachi; Hebrews 13:7-17

Acknowledgements

My sincerest thanks to my husband, Ryan, who has always taken seriously his role as pastor for our family, reading us God's Word daily. These family Bible readings have gotten me through dry spells, when I didn't personally read Scripture, due to exhaustion, new babies, and illness. He has also encouraged me in my vocation as full-time mother, sacrificing to allow me to stay at home with the children. He's also an excellent theologian for bouncing my ideas off of, and an amazing publishing partner.

I also thank my children for sacrificing time with me while I worked on this project. Through them, I have been given the opportunity to learn so much about motherhood and the application of God's Word in our lives, not to mention patience!

I'm grateful to my mom and dad for raising me in the faith, bringing me to the waters of baptism with Pastor Baerbock, teaching me and confirming me, and paying for 15 years of Christian education. Thanks, also, to my brother Adam for sharing his compilation of the hymn numbers from the different Lutheran hymnals.

Thanks, also, to my dear friends and editors. Anna Gullixson has given me invaluable Gospel-oriented suggestions, keeping me on the straight-and-narrow. Andy Waltz's eagle eyes helped me look for layout mistakes I didn't even know could be made! I'm grateful for both of their work to this labor of love.

Special thanks go out to Mary Moerbe for her patient correspondence and lovely foreword to the book. I also credit her father, Dr. Gene Veith, for first introducing me to the accessible Doctrine of Vocation in his book *God at Work,* 15 years ago.

Finally, I want to express my gratitude to all of my pastors and teachers throughout the years, in particular Pastor John Petersen and Professor Dennis Marzolf for their assistance on this book. To God be all glory!

Appendix 1: Luther's Small Catechism

The Commandments

The First Commandment

You shall have no other gods.

What does this mean?

We should fear, love and trust in God above all things.

The Second Commandment

You shall not take the name of the Lord, your God, in vain.

What does this mean?

We should fear and love God, so that we do not curse, swear, practice witchcraft, lie or deceive by His name, but call upon Him in every trouble, pray, praise and give thanks.

The Third Commandment

You shall keep the day of rest holy.

What does this mean?

We should fear and love God, so that we do not despise preaching and His Word, but hold it sacred and gladly hear and learn it.

The Fourth Commandment

Honor your father and your mother, that it may be well with you, and that you may live long on the earth.

What does this mean?

We should fear and love God, so that we do not despise our parents and superiors, nor provoke them to anger, but honor, serve, obey, love and esteem them.

The Fifth Commandment

You shall not kill.

What does this mean?

We should fear and love God, so that we do no bodily harm to our neighbor, but help and befriend him in every need.

The Sixth Commandment

You shall not commit adultery.

What does this mean?

We should fear and love God, so that we lead a chaste and decent life in word and deed, and that husband and wife each love and honor the other.

The Seventh Commandment

You shall not steal.

What does this mean?

We should fear and love God, so that we do not take our neighbor's money or goods, nor get them in any dishonest way, but help him to improve and protect his goods and means of making a living.

The Eighth Commandment

You shall not bear false witness against your neighbor.

What does this mean?

We should fear and love God, so that we do not lie about, betray or slander our neighbor, but excuse him, speak well of him, and put the best construction on everything.

The Ninth Commandment

You shall not covet your neighbor's house.

What does this mean?

We should fear and love God, so that we do not craftily seek to gain our neighbor's inheritance or home, nor get it by a show of right, but help and serve him in keeping it.

The Tenth Commandment

You shall not covet your neighbor's wife, nor his manservant, nor his maidservant, nor his cattle, nor anything that is his.

What does this mean?

We should fear and love God, so that we do not tempt, force or coax away from our neighbor his wife or his workers, but urge them to stay and do their duty.

Conclusion

What does God say about these commandments?

I the Lord your God am a jealous God, visiting the iniquity of the fathers upon the children to the third and fourth generation of those who hate Me, and showing mercy to thousands of those who love Me and keep My commandments.

What does this mean?

God threatens to punish all who transgress these commandments. Therefore we should fear His wrath and do nothing against these commandments. But He promises grace and every blessing to all who keep these commandments. Therefore we should also love and trust in Him and willingly do according to His commandments.

The Apostle's Creed

The First Article

I believe in God the Father Almighty, Maker of heaven and earth.

What does this mean?

I believe that God has made me and all creatures; that He has given me my body and soul, eyes, ears and all my members, my reason and all my senses, and still preserves them; that He richly and daily provides me with food and clothing, home and family, property and goods, and all that I need to support this body and life; that He protects me from all danger, guards and keeps me from all evil; and all this purely out of fatherly, divine goodness and mercy, without any merit or worthiness in me; for all which I am in duty bound to thank and praise, to serve and obey Him. This is most certainly true.

The Second Article

I believe in Jesus Christ, His only Son our Lord; Who was conceived by the Holy Spirit, born of the virgin Mary, suffered under Pontius Pilate, was crucified, died and was buried. He descended into hell; the third day He rose again from the dead; He ascended into heaven and is seated at the right hand of God the Father almighty; from there He shall come to judge the living and the dead.

What does this mean?

I believe that Jesus Christ is true God, begotten of the Father from eternity, and also true man, born of the virgin Mary; and that He is my Lord, Who has redeemed me, a lost and condemned creature, purchased and won me from all sins, from death and from the power of the devil; not with gold or silver, but with His holy, precious blood, and with His innocent suffering and death; in order that I might be His own, live under Him in His kingdom, and serve Him in everlasting righteousness, innocence and blessedness; even as He is risen from the dead, lives and reigns to all eternity. This is most certainly true.

The Third Article

I believe in the Holy Spirit, the holy Christian Church, the communion of saints, the forgiveness of sins, the resurrection of the body, and the life everlasting. Amen. What does this mean?

What does this mean?

I believe that I cannot by my own reason or strength believe in Jesus Christ, my Lord, or come to Him; but the Holy Ghost has called me by the Gospel, enlightened me with His gifts, sanctified and kept me in the true faith; just as He calls, gathers, enlightens and sanctifies the whole Christian Church on earth and keeps it with Jesus Christ in the one true faith. In this Christian Church He daily and richly forgives me and all believers all our sins; and at the last day He will raise up me and all the dead, and will grant me and all believers in Christ eternal life. This is most certainly true.

The Lord's Prayer

The Introduction

Our Father, Who art in heaven.

What does this mean?

God would hereby tenderly invite us to believe that He is our true Father, and that we are His true children, so that we may ask Him with all boldness and confidence, as children ask their dear father.

The First Petition

Hallowed be Thy name.

What does this mean?

God's name is certainly holy in itself, but we pray in this petition that it may be holy among us also.

How is God's name hallowed?

God's name is kept holy when His Word is taught in its truth and purity, and we as the children of God live holy lives according to it. This grant us, dear Father in heaven! But he who teaches and lives otherwise than the Word of God teaches dishonors God's name among us. From this preserve us, heavenly Father!

The Second Petition

Thy Kingdom come.

What does this mean?

The kingdom of God certainly comes of itself without our prayer, but we pray in this petition that it may come to us also.

How does God's kingdom come?

The kingdom of God comes when our heavenly Father gives us His Holy Spirit, so that by His grace we believe His holy Word and live godly lives here in time and hereafter in eternity.

The Third Petition

Thy will be done on earth, as it is in heaven.

What does this mean?

The good and gracious will of God is certainly done without our prayer, but we pray in this petition that it may be done also among us.

How is God's will done?

God's will is done when He breaks and hinders every evil counsel and will which would not let us hallow His name nor let His kingdom come, such as the will of the devil, the world and our own flesh; but strengthens and keeps us steadfast in His Word and in faith until our end. This is His good and gracious will.

The Fourth Petition

Give us this day our daily bread.

What does this mean?

God certainly gives daily bread without our prayer, even to all the wicked; but we pray in this petition that He would lead us to acknowledge this and to receive our daily bread with thanksgiving.

What is meant by daily bread?

Daily bread includes everything needed for this life, such as food, drink, clothing, shoes, house, home, fields, cattle, money, goods, God-fearing spouse and children, faithful servants and rulers, good government, good weather, peace, health, order, honor, true friends, good neighbors, and the like.

The Fifth Petition

And forgive us our trespasses, as we forgive those who trespass against us.

What does this mean?

We pray in this petition that our Father in heaven would not look upon our sins, nor on their account deny our prayer; for we are not worthy of anything we ask, neither have we deserved it. But we pray that He would give us everything by grace, for we daily sin much and deserve nothing but punishment; and we on our part will heartily forgive and readily do good to those who sin against us.

The Sixth Petition

And lead us not into temptation.

What does this mean?

God certainly tempts no one to sin, but we pray in this petition that God would guard and keep us so that the devil, the world and our own flesh may not deceive us nor lead us into misbelief, despair and other shameful sin and vice; and though we be thus tempted, that we may still in the end overcome and retain the victory.

The Seventh Petition

But deliver us from evil.

What does this mean?

We pray in this petition, as the sum of all, that our Father in heaven would deliver us from every evil of body and soul, property and honor; and at last, when the hour of death shall come, grant us a blessed end, and graciously take us from this valley of sorrow to Himself in heaven.

The Conclusion

For Thine is the kingdom, and the power, and the glory, forever and ever. Amen.

What does "Amen" mean?

Amen means that we should be sure that these petitions are acceptable to our Father in heaven and are heard by Him; for He himself has commanded us so to pray and has promised to hear us. Amen, Amen: that is, Yes, Yes, it shall be so.

Baptism

The Nature of Baptism

What is Baptism?

Baptism is not just water, but it is the water used according to God's command and connected with His Word.

What is that Word and command of God concerning Baptism?

Jesus says: "All authority has been given to Me in heaven and on earth. Go therefore and make disciples of all nations, baptizing them in the name of the Father and of the Son and of the Holy Spirit, teaching them to observe all things whatever I have commanded you." Matthew 28:18–20.

The Blessings of Baptism

What does Baptism give or profit?

Baptism effects forgiveness of sins, delivers from death and the devil, and gives eternal salvation to all who believe this, just as the words and promises of God declare.

Which are these words and promises of God?

Christ our Lord says, Mark 16:16: "He who believes and is baptized will be saved; but he who does not believe will be condemned."

The Power of Baptism

How can water do such great things?

It is not the water that does these things, but the Word of God which is in and with the water, and faith which trusts this Word of God in the water. For without the Word of God the water is simply water, and no baptism; but with the Word of God it is a baptism, that is, a gracious water of life and a washing of regeneration in the Holy Spirit, as St. Paul says, Titus 3:5–8: "According to His mercy He saved us, by the washing of regeneration and renewing of the Holy Spirit, whom He poured out on us abundantly through Jesus Christ our Savior; that having been justified by His grace, we should become heirs according to the hope of eternal life. This is a faithful saying."

The Meaning of Baptism

What does such baptizing with water mean?

Such baptizing with water means that the old Adam in us should, by daily contrition and repentance, be drowned and die with all sins and evil lusts; and that a new man daily come forth and arise, who shall live before God in righteousness and purity forever.

Where is this written?

St. Paul writes, Romans 6:4: "We are buried with Christ by baptism into death, that just as He was raised up from the dead by the glory of the Father, even so we also should walk in newness of life."

The Office of the Keys and Confession

What is the Office of the Keys?

The Office of the Keys is the special authority which Christ has given to His Church on earth: to forgive the sins of the penitent sinners, but to retain the sins of the impenitent as long as they do not repent.

Where is this written?

The evangelist writes, John 20:22–23: "Jesus breathed on His disciples and said to them, 'Receive the Holy Spirit. If you forgive the sins of any, they are forgiven them; and if you retain the sins of any, they are retained.'"

What is Confession?

Confession consists of two parts: one, that we confess our sins; the other, that we receive absolution, or forgiveness, from the pastor or confessor as from God himself, and in no way doubt, but firmly believe that our sins are thereby forgiven before God in heaven.

What sins should we confess?

Before God we should acknowledge ourselves guilty of all sins, even of those which we do not know about, as we do in the Lord's Prayer. But before the pastor or confessor we should acknowledge those sins only which we know and feel in our hearts.

Which are these?

Here consider your own situation according to the Ten Commandments, whether you are a father, mother, son, daughter, employer, employee; whether you have been disobedient, dishonest, lazy; whether you have injured anyone by word or deed; whether you have stolen, neglected, wasted anything, or done any harm.

The Sacrament of the Altar

The Nature of the Sacrament of the Altar

What is the Sacrament of the Altar?

The Sacrament of the Altar is the true body and blood of our Lord Jesus Christ, under the bread and wine, instituted by Christ himself, for us Christians to eat and to drink.

Where is this written?

The holy evangelists Matthew, Mark and Luke, together with St. Paul, write thus: "Our Lord Jesus Christ, the same night in which He was betrayed, took bread; and when He had given thanks, He broke it and gave it to His disciples, saying, 'Take, eat; this is My body, which is given for you. Do this in remembrance of Me.' In the same way also He took the cup after supper, gave thanks and gave it to them, saying, Drink from it, all of you; this cup is the New Testament in My blood, which is shed for you for the remission of sins. Do this, as often as you drink it, in remembrance of Me.'"

The Benefit of the Sacrament of the Altar

What benefit do we receive from such eating and drinking?

The benefit which we receive from such eating and drinking is shown us by these words: "Given and shed for you for the remission of sins," namely, that in the Sacrament forgiveness of sins, life and salvation are given us through these words. For where there is forgiveness of sins, there is also life and salvation.

The Power of the Sacrament of the Altar

How can bodily eating and drinking do such great things?

It is not the eating and drinking that does this, but the words here written: "Given and shed for you for the remission of sins." These words, along with the eating and drinking, are the main thing in the Sacrament; and whoever believes these words has exactly what they say, namely, the forgiveness of sins.

The Proper Reception of the Sacrament of the Altar

Who then receives this Sacrament worthily?

Fasting and bodily preparation are indeed a fine outward training; but he is truly worthy and well prepared who has faith in these words, "Given and shed for you for the remission of sins." But he who does not believe these words, or doubts them, is unworthy and unprepared; for the words "for you" require truly believing hearts.

Reprinted, with permission, from
www.els.org/beliefs/luthers-small-catechism

Appendix 2: Hymnal Conversion Chart

Compiled by Adam Holtz,
adapted from a list by Richard Mau in 1998

The following chart will assist you in finding the melody, in your own hymnal, of the *ELH* hymns that have been selected for each devotion, indexed at p. 192. Alternatively, you may consult the metrical index in your own hymnal to find a suitable tune that matches the rhythm of the hymn you are seeking to sing.

ELH	*Evangelical Lutheran Hymnary* (1996)
CW	*Christian Worship* (1992)
LSB	*Lutheran Service Book* (2006)
LW	*Lutheran Worship* (1982)
LHy	*Lutheran Hymnary* (1913)
TLH	*The Lutheran Hymnal* (1941)

ELH	CW	LSB	LW	LHy	TLH
1	221	904	202	34	16
2	176	497	154	375	224
3					
4			247		
5					
6	241	822	437		23
7			387		
8	531	909		129	466
9		501	162		
10	177	498	157	355	233

ELH	CW	LSB	LW	LHy	TLH
11				382	227
12	193	905	169	73	239
13				37	
14				40	8
15	195	507	168	72	246
16	250	816	440	21	15
17					
18	192	505	170		247
19					51
20				381	

ELH	CW	LSB	LW	LHy	TLH
21					
22					
23	230	902	201	36	3
24	282	908	197		5
25	185	693	336	18	293
26				380	
27	184	913	160	374	235
28				45	
29	255	901	198	35	1
30	255	901	198	35	1
31	229				12
32	225	903	200		10
33	190	768	155		231
34	266	942	209		6
35	263	947	215	2	237
36	262	948	210		238
37	271	953	212	76	252
38	270	954	213	71	251
39					
40	267	960	214		249
41	268	434	208	147	146
42	277				
43	278	940	171		250
44				1	
45					

ELH	CW	LSB	LW	LHy	TLH
46		936			
47	274				275
48	269	938	185		137
49	370	549	272	6	339
50					
51	233	791	435		14
52					581
53	344	512	178		
54	369	537	507	576	657
55	341	525	278		341
56	252		205	11	44
57	430	726	419		
58				26	
59		738			
60	238	814	457	65	27
61	364				
62				459	
63	610	895	443	31	36
64				12	
65	234	790	444	5	39
66	227	812	204		344
67		793		9	
68				128	
69	76	102	76	41	57
70					

ELH	CW	LSB	LW	LHy	TLH
71			456		33
72	280	578	328		
73					
74	582	868	478	539	536
75		872			539
76	581	875	482		
77	590	877	492	544	549
78					547
79					548
80	584	876	479		541
81	586	874	481		550
82	478	869	483		540
83					542
84				22	
85	251	807	460		
86	585				544
87	6	338	22	202	
88	8	350	34		55
89	26	353			56
90	2	332	13	186	95
91	3	341	24	158	73
92	4	340	23	158	73
93					
94				157	
95				160	

ELH	CW	LSB	LW	LHy	TLH
96	15	345	18	164	60
97	22	355	32		
98	29	336	15	166	
99	1	331	12		68
100	10	514	176		67
101	25	348	26		
102	11	347	28	170	61
103	93	398	82	168	59
104	134	335	20	161	57
105				162	69
106	16	344	14	176	63
107	20	346	187		272
108		351		174	
109	12	349	29	175	66
110	23	357	1,31	172	62
111	32			173	65
112				194	
113	36	383	51	182	76
114	80	367	50	192	136
115	37	360	39	177	77
116	63	368	55		
117			66		
118	44				
119	68	364	64		
120					

ELH	CW	LSB	LW	LHy	TLH
121	47	359	67		645
122					107
123	38	358	37	181	85
124	38	358	38	181	85
125	61	380	49	198	94
126					
127	51		56		
128	42	375	48		90
129					
130					
131					78
132				197	
133	55	379	41	195	102
134	64	390	42		97
135	34	386	47	199	92
136				184	
137	65	361	60	196	647
138	62	387	53	201	87
139	50	376	58		
140	60	363	68	178	646
141	17	333	30		74
142	49	391	520	183	79
143				193	
144	46			179	
145	67	370	61		

ELH	CW	LSB	LW	LHy	TLH
146	48				
147			70	188	109
148	41	389	44		105
149	346	818	442		
150				185	
151	78				138
152					108
153	90	412	77		106
154	53		52		103
155	358	524	279	417	364
156	76	900	182	211	114
157					115
158		898			117
159					116
160	441	733	180	212	123
161	40	372			81
162					
163	45	897	40		96
164					99
165	28	352	33		91
166	81	396	85		126
167	79	395	73	220	343
168	83	397	75	219	127
169	92	400	86	224	128
170	85	810	83	122	132

ELH	CW	LSB	LW	LHy	TLH
171	279	523	335	134	294
172	82	394	88		134
173	91	399	81		131
174	449	725			
175		392			
176	509		474	573	286
177	432	740	517		648
178	510		476		655
179		588			
180	512	867	472		629
181	35	384	36		98
182	290	536	277	227	366
183	515	864	471	574	628
184	402	702	378	456	394
185		410	80	228	133
186	516		473		630
187	501	863	465		
188	603				
189	503		466	229	624
190	506	862	467	234	625
191	573	826	318	121	496
192				93	487
193	84	832	312	117	511
194	579	837	311		
195	557	835	320		

ELH	CW	LSB	LW	LHy	TLH
196					
197	382	575	368	236	370
198	569	839	314	221	512
199	577				498
200		510	464	239	415
201	576	830	321	119	507
202			317	123	508
203					
204	450				
205	444	750	420	230	518
206	446	729	408		428
207	395	557	358		383
208				284	
209	357		508	244	345
210	439	722	512		
211	529	645	291	132	467
212	536	647	293		477
213					269
214		648	294	88	469
215				245	
216					
217				87	472
218				70	
219					406
220	461				411

ELH	CW	LSB	LW	LHy	TLH
221					265
222	380	573			37
223	96	413	87	253	
224	86	402	72	167	
225				249	
226	384	566	351		373
227	390	555	355	205	377
228	324	577	342	261	49
229					
230	283	589	339	260	296
231					
232	284		332		285
233	288	580	330		297
234	291		340		290
235	101			265	165
236	452	685	381		409
237				274	
238				587	
239	372	606	366	439	652
240	108	423	90	264	145
241	299	601	225	141	301
242	294	590	224		298
243					
244	295	592	226		300
245					

ELH	CW	LSB	LW	LHy	TLH
246		594			
247	88	406	223		
248					
249	457	664	299	258	447
250	200	656	298	270	262
251	201	657	297	270	262
252	431	716	391	269	413
253	472	663	302	409	446
254					
255				275	
256				277	
257	413	615	428	524	522
258	362			278	353
259				280	
260					
261	447	714	414	282	437
262	331	918	220	285	54
263	349	743	270	351	347
264	349	743	270	351	347
265					
266				287	
267	39	385	43	291	104
268				290	
269					
270	351	531	284	303	367

ELH	CW	LSB	LW	LHy	TLH
271	27				328
272					
273		455	2		168
274				464	
275				308	
276	109		367		152
277	131	442	102		160
278	373	554	274	292	361
279	130	443	106		161
280	132	441	105	293	162
281	371	544	275		
282	129	437	97	318	154
283	103	433	98		158
284	104	436	110	304	159
285					169
286	389	761	361	27	376
287	98	440	109		140
288					
289	359				220
290					
291				584	148
292	117	439	119	300	143
293	121	421	95	297	144
294				320	
295				302	

ELH	CW	LSB	LW	LHy	TLH
296	124	419	93	305	166
297	127	451	116	316	153
298	122	454	117		
299					
300	111			323	155
301	112		506	314	157
302		561			
303	110	430	91		
304	113	453	120		171
305	128	431	99		156
306	120	543			
307					
308	125	425	115	306	175
309					304
310	141	633	126		
311		623	250		314
312					
313	310	618	242		315
314	309	637	240	150	307
315				154	350
316	313	627	236		311
317	313	627	237		311
318				419	
319	397	570	359	447	388
320	312	622	246		306

ELH	CW	LSB	LW	LHy	TLH
321				311	
322		625	248		312
323				153	
324					
325	316	632	245	155	309
326	314	642	244	148	316
327	317	617	238	156	313
328	311	636	239	149	305
329	135	634	107		163
330				321	
331	100	438	111	301	142
332	137	448	122	322	167
333	114	420	94		151
334	105	450	113	315	172
335	105	449	113	315	172
336				319	
337			108		177
338					
339					
340	153			326	188
341	156	467	128		192
342					
343	161	458	123	330	195
344	155			334	190
345	150	463	137		191

ELH	CW	LSB	LW	LHy	TLH
346					
347	142	487	141	328	204
348	162	488	520	329	189
349					
350	143	480	138		198
351	152	461	264	332	200
352	157	457	127		199
353	145	490	139	331	201
354	147	548		325	207
355					
356	166	478	133	327	205
357	148	464	143	324	210
358	164		136		
359	265	155	p161		
360	151		144		
361	404			337	
362					365
363	356	526	283	339	355
364	405			243	396
365				341	217
366	165	470	130		208
367	508		475	575	627
368				345	
369					
370	375	709	412	420	431

ELH	CW	LSB	LW	LHy	TLH
371	360	710	416		436
372	479	683	280	347	349
373					
374	393	568			375
375		666	300	85	263
376			179	348	
377	428	756	423	342	523
378	377	556	353	526	387
379	348			353	348
380	248	796	449		
381	409	779	433	16	459
382	412			360	
383	410	766	431	359	458
384				4	
385	411	770	516	488	457
386					
387				361	454
388	175				213
389	171	493	149		212
390					
391				367	214
392	173	492	150		216
393	217	532		365	219
394					223
395	567		315	116	494

ELH	CW	LSB	LW	LHy	TLH
396	202			527	267
397		553	151	373	
398	179	489	125		
399	180			383	230
400				266	228
401		503	163	379	
402	183	496	166		234
403	391	571	352		245
404		794	174		38
405					
406	434	708	413	393	429
407	365	700	286	295	351
408					
409	476	694	375	474	399
410	239	506	173		244
411					282
412	106	435	96	399	149
413	336	684	345	514	276
414	445	746	369		372
415	437		357	96	319
416	383				392
417	308	614	235	401	331
418				406	
419					
420	494	649	295		464

ELH	CW	LSB	LW	LHy	TLH
421				407	
422	453	688	379		421
423	460	703	385		417
424	465			408	423
425					
426	304	609	229	411	324
427	596	689	257	410	334
428	527				
429	385	611	285		342
430					
431	396	569	292		
432	376	563	362	415	371
433		567		414	389
434	420	765	426	421	514
435	236	819	452	3	19
436	191	504	175	75	240
437				418	
438	181		165	426	226
439		659	301	84	258
440	205			424	260
441	462	707	392	425	416
442					
443	242	811	448	443	30
444	469	783	404		400
445	485	781	405		441

ELH	CW	LSB	LW	LHy	TLH
446	477	730	418		430
447	480				438
448	253		439	436	25
449				434	
450	302	608	233	497	326
451				440	378
452	305	607	230	273	329
453					327
454	423			522	
455	303			441	323
456	257	820	453	7	34
457				455	
458	499	852	397	450	439
459	486	851	402	449	442
460		559	364		384
461	613	892	495	532	574
462				453	525
463				529	
464	614	893	493	530	
465	418	713	409	349	393
466	609		494		568
467	438	745	421		526
468	421	732	415		425
469					
470	459	696	371	457	395

ELH	CW	LSB	LW	LHy	TLH
471	347		393	369	346
472					601
473	606	742	267	583	597
474	417	748	515	462	660
475				600	
476				594	
477	435	758	425		517
478	605			593	587
479					
480					
481				582	594
482				248	
483	210			579	598
484				81	
485		906	203	471	9
486	538	644	289	78	473
487				444	
488					
489	286				289
490	285	581	331		287
491	378	562	363		369
492	287	579	329	416	295
493	306	613	234	97	318
494	403	587	354		381
495				101	330

ELH	CW	LSB	LW	LHy	TLH
496		610	231	103	320
497	235	797	445		26
498					
499	386		360	478	385
500				99	325
501	543	682	258		483
502			261	95	489
503					485
504					
505	548				493
506	456	854	380		
507	545	681	263		491
508					332
509				108	
510				110	
511	541	585	344	427	292
512				111	336
513	598		255		335
514	599			106	337
515	426	687	256	107	338
516				430	
517	419	724	407	272	528
518	455	668	303	165	444
519	429	760	422	370	521
520					501

ELH	CW	LSB	LW	LHy	TLH
521	416	728	411	340	427
522					321
523	345	427	101	262	354
524	448	734	406		524
525	211			506	592
526	554	679	268	596	589
527	534	755	265		590
528					599
529					
530	608				585
531				437	
532	167	741	266	509	206
533	289	658	337		264
534		513	463	608	605
535					407
536				603	
537	209			601	607
538	207	508	462		611
539	215	673	307	609	618
540		670	308		475
541	212	674	306	610	619
542				263	
543	7	515		602	72
544	206	516	177	508	609
545	196	522	189		254

ELH	CW	LSB	LW	LHy	TLH
546	198				256
547					257
548		520	190		255
549	204		341		266
550					268
551	514	865	477		288
552	213			618	616
553	550	676	192	492	656
554	551	677	191		463
555					470
556					259
557				617	476
558	552	517	193	494	
559		661	304	491	452
560	589		491	562	654
561	588	878	490	552	552
562					563
563				333	194
564					
565	592	883	484	560	558
566					
567		881			
568					
569	587	880	485	551	554
570	593	887	503		653

ELH	CW	LSB	LW	LHy	TLH
571		882		557	559
572		888	486		101
573				585	600
574	591	890	487		564
575				554	
576	504		469		643
577			488	566	551
578					197
579	333	919	287	57	53
580	323	923	216	56	52
581	170	701	153	58	215
582	249				20
583	293	582	333	137	283
584	522	777	219		
585				50	
586	325		222	46	48
587	422	718	386	505	410
588	329	924	218	48	50
589	203	655	334	138	261
590				52	
591	574	823	288	29	500
592	334	805	461		644
593	319	422	100	298	179
594	322	921	217		46
595				49	

ELH	CW	LSB	LW	LHy	TLH
596	470	692	387	53	401
597	321	917	221	54	47
598	320	422	100	298	179
599	616	774	468		659
600				568	
601				569	
602	619	965	497	519	577

Appendix 3: Recommended Resources

Websites

Concordian Sisters of Perpetual Parturtion

www.concordiansisters.blogspot.com

> Though no longer an active blog, these authors offer many Scriptural, thought-provoking insights on motherhood.

The Hausvater Project

www.hausvater.org

> "Equipping fathers and mothers to meet their children's spiritual needs." There are many great devotional resources here.

Into Your Hands LLC

www.intoyourhandsllc.com

> Into Your Hands LLC specializes in research, consulting, publishing, training, and advocacy consistent with natural law. Marie also blogs at Into Your Hands LLC.

Sister, Daughter, Mother, Wife

www.sisterdaughtermotherwife.com

> "Sister, Daughter, Mother, Wife is an online source of Lutheran encouragement, community, and advice. This is where you can find discussions of relationships in a Law and Gospel context. Topics range from living the single life, to building cross-generational friendships, to teaching children to behave respectfully in church."

Books

Alcorn, Randy. *The Goodness of God: Assurance of Purpose in the Midst of Suffering*. Portland: Multnomah, 2010.

This wonderful book gives a Biblical perspective for anyone struggling with pain, grief, or loss.

Curtis, Rebekah and Adle, Rose. *LadyLike: Living Biblically*. St. Louis: Concordia, 2015.

This book is filled with essays about Biblical femininity.

MacPherson, Marie. *Mothering Many: Sanity-Saving Strategies from Moms of Four or More*. Mankato, Minn.: Into Your Hands, LLC, 2016.

Mothering Many is filled with practical ideas for managing a large household.

MacPherson, Ryan. *Studying Luther's Large Catechism: A Workbook for Christian Discipleship*. Mankato, Minn.: The Hausvater Project, 2012.

This study guide is an accessible way for individuals or groups to dive into Luther's Large Catechism.

Moldstad, Joslyn W. *At Home with Jesus: Devotions for Children*. Milwaukee: Northwestern Publishing House, 1992.

Mrs. Moldstad's book provides Gospel-centered devotions for families.

Pawlitz, Gail. *The Story Bible*. St. Louis: Concordia, 2011.

Beautifully illustrated, this story book uses words directly from Scripture.

Veith, Gene Edward. *The Spirituality of the Cross: The Way of the First Evangelicals*. St. Louis: Concordia, 2010.

This book is a primer on the theology of Lutherans.

———. *God at Work: Your Christian Vocation in All of Life*. Wheaton, Ill.: Crossway, 2011.

This is an excellent introduction to the Doctrine of Vocation, and the first book which exposed me to it.

Veith, Gene Edward and Mary J. Moerbe. *Family Vocation: God's Calling in Marriage, Parenting, and Childhood*. Wheaton, Ill.: Crossway, 2012.

Dr. Veith and his daughter, Mary, team up to apply the Doctrine of Vocation to Christian families. See also my dialogue with Mary at:
www.intoyourhandsllc.com/blog/151

Appendix 4: Personal Writings

When Mother is Dispensable

It was a beautiful dream come true: finishing school, getting married to her college sweetheart, becoming pregnant. It wasn't an easy pregnancy by any means, though. So much morning sickness. Except that it wasn't morning sickness at all. My friend's son was delivered by C-section at 28 weeks, so she could begin treatment for stomach cancer as soon as possible. She had a few more months with her son and husband before she left this world, and thanks be to Christ, into the arms of her Heavenly Father.

My friend was safely home. What about her little boy? Family, friends, and the community came together to help the father and lift him up in his difficult vocation of single fatherhood, all the while still mourning for that beautiful dream. Before long, God provided a new wife for this man, and a new mother for his son. I recently saw this lovely family with their active 4-year-old son, his new little sister, and another baby on the way.

During her medical ordeal, I checked my friend's Facebook page frequently for updates. I talked to fellow church members to hear if there was any news. I hugged my own children a little more tightly. And I realized that I am dispensable.

Wait. What?

As Lutherans, we've got a lot of good theology going for us, including the Doctrine of Vocation and the proper distinction of the roles of men and women. We value females for being what God made them to be, not just for their education, ambitions, or climb up the corporate ladder. We posit that children need both fathers and mothers and that mothers have a unique and irreplaceable role in raising their babies. So, why would an author who believes all that call mothers dispensable?

God grants the blessing of children and the vocation of motherhood. He handpicks parents for children. He chooses to provide for the young and the old primarily through their families.

But He can and sometimes does choose to bless our families in creative and unique ways.

We as women, whether sisters, daughters, mothers, or wives, have all had situations where we just couldn't do it. There was a project we couldn't accomplish. There was sickness which made us incompetent to fill our role. There was a failure that let down our loved ones. But life still went on. Apologies were made and forgiveness was given.

Turns out, we didn't have to do it all. In fact, we can't do it all. In *Eternal Treasures*, Mary Moerbe explains it in these words: "God does not depend on parental competency in order to raise a child [or serve our families]....We might feel like we need to be in control, but a beautiful, gracious thing is already at work, helping us and raising our children: God's Word" (p. 99).

God is good. He doesn't leave us in the sins of our parents, Adam and Eve, or in our own wickedness. He promised a Savior, and he fulfilled that promise. This was no project He couldn't accomplish; no sickness left Him incompetent; no failure let us down. He provided the obedience, death, and resurrection of Jesus, that through Him, we may have life more abundantly (John 10:10).

I learned so much from my friend, in both life and death. Her trial and death taught me that even if I die, God will continue to care for the physical and spiritual needs of my children. Doesn't it follow that He will also care for them if I'm just not as capable as I hoped I would be? There will be cycles of times in our lives when we as servants to our families can't do what we are "supposed" to be doing. But, despite our inadequacies, God can still provide in creative and merciful ways.

Take heart, mothers, sisters, daughters, and wives! God planned for your presence in your family in this moment, even if it means your family must serve you in this season. Even if it has become your vocation to receive, rather than give. Even in the last dark walk through the valley of the shadow of death. God can and will provide for your children and family, both spiritually and physically, with or without you. Your children (and you) are baptized into Christ, children of Paradise. Nothing can snatch them out of His hand.

Reprinted, with permission, from
www.sisterdaughtermotherwife.com/2016/06/when-mother-is-
dispensable.html

Mama, Do You Remember?

Do you remember when I was two months old, I suddenly refused to drink your milk? You had no idea why, but you continued to try to nurse me. I insistently continued to refuse. You gave up, disappointed. But you continued to compassionately care for me. Even though there wasn't extra money, you found a creative way to get me nutritious milk. It was from that experience you taught me that life is full of disappointments, but also creative ways of overcoming those difficulties.

Do you remember when I was barely able to toddle around the front yard, you gave me my very first memory: Swinging back and forth on a wooden slab of a tree swing, with you in front of me, you pushing me back, and waiting with a kiss on my cheek every swing forward? I learned the value of unconditional love.

Do you remember when I was a little girl, still with my baby curls, you would take a break from all of your housework, and sit and color *The Bear Family Coloring Book* with me at the dining room table? We would pick out fresh pages in which there was no coloring on either side, so we could each color one half of the spread. I would always give you the prettiest blue from my crayon box, because that was your favorite. I learned the joy of companionship in the little things.

Do you remember when I was a child, we were separated all day from each other by school and work? You would be exhausted from your medical transcriptionist job. But you were never too tired to come to my room and read me a Bible story (if you asked me to choose, I always picked Daniel in the Lions' Den) and say my prayers with me. It was then that I learned the importance of faith in God and consistency in devotions.

Do you remember when I was in grade school and I got parts in a few plays, like *Little House on the Prairie, Snow White*, and *The Wizard of Oz*? You committed to make costumes for me and coach me with my lines, over and over again, even when you had them memorized and could have played the part for me! I learned the value of support, encouragement, and hard work.

Do you remember when I was carving my entry for the Pine Car Derby? I came home that terrible night from Lutheran Girl Pioneers. I could hear Dad on the phone in the background. You were taxed with the horrific task of explaining the tragic death of Aunt Rose and cousins Theresa, Tina, and Timothy in the car accident. It was then that I learned that it is okay to cry and cling and hurt, all while fully trusting in Jesus.

Do you remember that special promise you made me before I started my first cycle? You promised I could choose something exceptional to plan and look forward to, when the time came. And when it did, you delivered the anticipated helicopter ride at the county fair. I learned the value of life changes, for better and for worse.

I'll never forget the night you lost your temper and scared me terribly because of your depression. Nor will I ever forget how you handled it afterward, sitting on my bed with me as I completed my science fair project, apologizing profusely and telling me how sorry you were. It was then that I learned the value of admitting my own fears and mistakes and humbly asking for forgiveness.

Do you remember the day before I started freshman year? You drove away crying from the boarding high school campus, devastated to be leaving me, all because you thought it was the best way for me to have a Christian education. Then, I learned that it can be okay to have a broken heart for a higher purpose.

Do you remember when I was home for summer break from school, and had looked forward for weeks to going to a Rebecca St. James concert with one of my few close friends? When she ditched me a few short hours before the show, you not only canceled your own country music concert with your friends (including losing the money from the cost of the non-refundable ticket) so you could comfort me. You even came up with the idea of attending my own concert with me, and never once complained! We waved our hands and praised "Our God Is an Awesome God" under a starry sky. I learned the value of sacrifice for those you love.

Do you remember the day I was dressed in white from veil to heel (and you were pretty in pink)? You hugged me with tears in your eyes and, lips quivering, said that Ryan was a good man, a blessing from the Lord, and now you would entrust my care to Him. I learned the value of letting go and giving control to God.

Do you remember the day when I became a mother? You were there, a silent observer in a sterile background, when Grace took her first breath (after 43 hours of being shy)! Oh how glad I am that you were there, though I hadn't expected you and didn't think I wanted you there! After seeing the astonishment in your eyes from this unique experience (that has not been erased from your memory, as so many things now have) I truly learned the value of all life.

Do you remember when I was healing after the birth? You were invaluable in caring for both mother and child, even though I had previously said that I didn't think you would be needed afterward. How wrong I was! It was then that I learned that my perceptions are often wrong, and so much good can come out of an unexpected situation.

Do you remember when we shared a pew and an embrace and a tissue box and sang "I'm But a Stranger Here" and "In the Garden" at the funerals of both your mother and father, within days of one another? As I held your orphaned hand, with the same lines and pattern that I had memorized long ago, I noticed that it had suddenly become like the hand of my own grandmother that I had once held and memorized decades earlier, a hand I could no longer hold.

Now, my own age is older than the age you were during most of my childhood memories. I myself have become a mother and am teaching my children these same generational lessons, lessons that are taught with much more than words, without even knowing I am teaching them. Just like you taught me, whether or not you remember. And now, you, my own mother, have truly showed me your humble vulnerability and need. You have asked me to be your mother. It is one of the most profound paradoxes known to mankind. But it isn't some abstract philosophical paradox. It is mine.

Your dementia has left you a widow and orphan in many ways. But the Lord sets the lonely in families. Now, you will be part of my family again as we welcome you to our home, with my husband, and children, and me. I am scared of this unknown. What will it be like to be a mother to you? What does motherhood even mean?

And then, I remember.

I remember what you yourself taught me through your example: Motherhood is compassion, and disappointment, and creatively overcoming difficulties. Motherhood is unconditional love and the joy of companionship in the little things. Motherhood should be demonstrating faith in God and consistency in devotions. Motherhood is support, encouragement, and hard work. It is okay to cry and cling and hurt, all while fully trusting in Jesus. Motherhood is valuing life changes, for better and for worse. Motherhood is admitting my own fears and mistakes and humbly asking for forgiveness. It can be okay to have a broken heart for a higher purpose. Motherhood is sacrifice and letting go and giving control to God. Motherhood is valuing all life. Motherhood is learning that my perceptions are often wrong, and so much good can come out of an unexpected situation.

You often forget, and perhaps you will forget more and more. But now, it is my turn to do for you as you have so graciously done for me, with the help of our awesome God. Now, I will creatively feed you nutritious food, and I will kiss your cheek (and perhaps it will be your last memory). I will sit with you to color, in the same Bear Family coloring book that I have saved all these years, and hand you the prettiest blue from my own babies' crayon box because it gives you joy from companionship. I will read God's Word with you and pray and sing hymns (and will remind you of your confirmation verse, "Be faithful unto death and I will give you the crown of life"). I will give you support and encouragement as you do your hard work of remembering. Together, we will cry and cling and hurt over your memory loss, all while fully trusting in Jesus. We will go through this life change together, for better and for worse. I'll probably lose my temper, and will need to humbly ask for your forgiveness. It's okay for us both to have a broken heart over your disability. Now, I will ditch my own plans —to sacrifice for you. I will let go, and give my life to God to care for you, because this is so obviously what He wants for our family. I can be all of this to you because God's strength is made perfect in weakness. In His wisdom, He has purposed from all eternity that He would give me you for my mother to teach me to be a mother, so I could be a mother for you.

During these hard, but happy years, I will often hold your hand that I had memorized long ago. Everyday, it will become a little bit more like the hand of your own mother. Someday, I will let go of your hand, and your care, and I will give you back to God in eternity. And my heart will be broken. And my children will hold my orphaned hand, which looks more like their grandmother's every day, and together we will cry and cling and hurt, all while fully trusting in Jesus. But that time is not yet. And I can go on, both now and then, because of the promise that Jesus is preparing a place for us, all of us. Someday, my own hand will join yours and Grandma's in Heaven in the holed-hands of our all-knowing, all-loving Savior, who will whisper to us all, "Well done, good and faithful servant! Come and share your Master's happiness." And finally, there will be no more tears, and no more forgetting.

Reprinted, with permission, from
www.intoyourhandsllc.com/blog/62

The Story of Baby Shalom

Upon first rising, on my oldest daughter's eleventh birthday, I took a pregnancy test. It was positive, and I was thrilled! And filled with trepidation. Does anyone ever feel truly prepared for the awesome responsibility of raising (another) precious child of God?

We shared our news with the children while taking their pictures to capture their reaction. ("Smile! We're having a new baby!") We let a few close family members and friends know. In the meantime, we've been trying to decide between various baby announcement ideas: an Easter basket with six eggs? A Pumpkin Pie that we're grateful to receive? (We're due at Thanksgiving.) A family of matryoshka dolls with a tiny one in the Mama? Something with kilts or bagpipes to celebrate our Scottish ancestry?

Things were going well. I didn't feel sick and had a lot of energy. Maybe too much? The pregnancy was very similar to the pregnancy I experienced in 2011, which ended sooner than expected with our miscarriage of Baby Selah. But...I tried to stay positive and pray for the best.

> "Cast all your anxiety on [the Lord] because He cares for you."
> 1 Peter 5:7

Now, it's Friday morning. I'm experiencing excruciating cramps, and bleeding almost imperceptibly. But throughout the day, while the cramping lessens, the bleeding picks up. I remember from Baby Selah's miscarriage, that if I call a healthcare provider, they will say there is nothing that can be done. But it feels wrong to do nothing. Surely, I should seek medical help if my baby is at risk? I take another pregnancy test. It is still positive. We still have hope.

I call my midwife on the phone, the same office which assisted me at my homebirths for my last two deliveries. The midwife assured me that many women spot during the first trimester and everything is fine for both the mother and child.

However, even if I would lose the baby, most women go on to have successful pregnancies after miscarriage.

So, what exactly is a "successful" pregnancy? Does it end in the birth of a healthy child? But what about all of the pregnancies that don't end that way? What about all of the heartbreaks, the babies given back to God? Are they failures? If so, then I have no influence over the outcome of success, because this is all out of my realm and in God's hands. A truly successful pregnancy is that in which I and my baby faithfully carry out the vocation of mother and child that God has put before us, until He ends that vocation, in whatever way or timing He has planned for His eternal glory.

> *"He who has begun a good work in you will complete it until the day of Jesus Christ." Philippians 1:6*

Vocation is defined as the roles in which God serves through people as a channel of His blessings. Surely I can be blessed through my child, and my child through me, even barring a healthy, no-incident nine-month pregnancy. Perhaps I might even be blessed more through suffering a loss? I acknowledge that His definition of success might be different than the world's.

> *"We also glory in our sufferings, because we know that suffering produces perseverance; perseverance, character; and character, hope." Romans 5:3–4*

I hang up with the midwife. Going to the hospital could only confirm that the baby remained alive, but it couldn't help if the baby had already died. I go to bed, not to the hospital, because I do not want to see my dead baby on a screen. I want to have hope. Hope that everything's okay, and I can wake up in the morning with no ill symptoms.

I wake up in the morning, vaguely aware of cramping. As I wake up more fully, I realize the severity of the cramps. I run to the bathroom, bleeding. I hunt throughout the bathroom, finding only one remaining pad. I didn't think I was going to need any for about seven and a half more months. Not a one in stock.

I know that I should just send my husband to the store, but our fridge is empty, and we need groceries, too. While I could certainly entrust the responsibility of pad-buying to my husband, I'm not willing to entrust him with the next week's worth of groceries since I do all of the cooking (from scratch). So, I prepare to go to the store.

As I walk through the store, trying not to keel over from the abdominal pain, I know I'm not here just for the pads or the groceries, but because I desperately feel the need to cling to a facade of normalcy—that everything is fine. But I'm not fine.

So, when the cashier asks, innocently, "How's your day going?" I do not answer, "I think I may be carrying death in my body. These pads, they aren't for my period. And I'm glad I'm wearing a long coat because I'm pretty sure that's blood pouring in a gush right now." I pay nonchalantly enough, holding back tears.

There's no way I'm going to make it home with the sorry state of my pants. I high-tail it to the grocery store bathroom with my rumpled plastic grocery bag of super-size pads under my arm, looking quite crazed, probably. I try to make myself at home in the tiny restroom stall. I sit, and suddenly feel the urge to bear down, and I do it, without thinking. A large clot falls into the toilet.

A moment later, I wonder. Is my baby in that clot? No. No, no, no! It's not supposed to happen like this! If I am going to miscarry, I want to see the precious baby's form, like Selah, and bury it in a tiny box in our backyard. I cannot give birth to my child and flush it down a filthy public toilet!

And, as my heart cries out in protest, I suddenly feel peace. It is no more difficult for God, the Almighty Maker of Heaven and Earth and all living beings, to resurrect a baby from a watery sewer than from a rotting grave in the earth.

> *"I believe in the resurrection of the dead,*
> *and the life of the world to come."*

The ultimate confession of this faith was not made at my confirmation, or weekly recitation in worship services, but with a simple, undignified flush of a toilet, commending the contents to the Heavenly Father, who hurts with me, but also reassures me of His love.

> *"I have loved you with an everlasting love; I have drawn you with unfailing kindness." Jeremiah 31:3*

I leave the bathroom, wondering. I'm concerned about the baby, but myself, too. I'm bleeding too much. I decide to go in to Urgent Care. They transfer me to the ER and my husband meets me there. The medical personnel plan to take a complete blood count, including measuring hCG levels for the pregnancy hormone, as well as taking both abdominal and trans-vaginal ultrasounds. My bleeding has significantly lessened by now, but I feel foggy and nauseated.

> *"Trust in the Lord with all your heart and lean not on your own understanding. In all your ways acknowledge Him and He will make your paths straight." Proverbs 3:5–6*

I put my feet up high in the stirrups for the ultrasound. This feels so strange, so foreign, after having two homebirths! I think to myself with relief, "I'm so glad I don't have to give birth like this!" And then I remember, I might actually be giving birth. The ultrasound tech tells us she isn't allowed to tell us a single thing about the pictures she is taking. She can't really even show us the pictures. I guess I'm thankful that I won't have to see my dead baby on the screen, right? But even a picture would be something! I have nothing. I am at my most vulnerable. And there might not even be a baby to hold at the end of this. Last night, and every night, I prayed,

> *"Into Your hands I commend myself. My body and soul and all things. Let Your holy angel be with me."*

As I wait, I think. To truly love means to be vulnerable to brokenness. To confess with my body my willingness to love another child by being open to conception is to be vulnerable to the pain of loss. This is nothing new. I'm not the first mother to experience loss. How can I expect any less, when my aim as a Christian is to pattern my life after the love of a Father who experienced the loss of His Son. For me. For my child.

"For me to live is Jesus, to die is gain." Philippians 1:21

And for my baby, too. Even if everything in my flesh shouts and fights for life on earth because it is all I know and understand, my heart and soul know that Heaven is my, and my children's, home.

The doctor comes into the room to give us the results. The ultrasound tech could not find an image of our baby. This could mean three possible things. 1) The baby has already died and passed out of my body. 2) The baby is fine, but it is either too small to see or is hiding where they couldn't see it. 3) Or I remain pregnant, but the baby is not growing in my womb, but some other dangerous part of my abdomen.

They cannot know until 48 hours from now, when I will take another blood test and they can compare the hCG levels. If they are higher than now, I remain pregnant and #3 is the most likely possibility. If they are lower than they are now, I have an empty womb and our child is already in Heaven.

Since my bleeding has practically stopped, they prepare to discharge me home from the ER. As I walk out to our car, I think it's not just that this situation is in God's hands, the baby is literally in God's hands. How strange to go home, not knowing the physical location of my child. But I know the baby is not lost. It is either in God's knitting hands, or in God's eternal hands.

"Peace I leave with you, My peace I give to you; not as the world gives do I give to you. Let not your heart be troubled, neither let it be afraid." John 14:27

We go home to tell the children. My oldest child listens carefully. I know this will not be the last time she also will feel vulnerability and brokenness for having loved. She makes the sign of the cross over my belly. My four-year-old says, "I will be sad and miss the baby if it is in Heaven. But when my life is done, I can be with the baby in Heaven!" O, for the faith of a child. We do our devotions and sing our evening hymn:

> *Let my near and dear ones be*
> *Always near and dear to Thee.*
> *Oh bring me and all I love*
> *To Thy happy home above.*

Thank you, God, for allowing me to bear another life. You give, you take away, blessed be Your name. You've given me the gift of vulnerability and brokenness to become more Christ-like in suffering. You help me appreciate through this experience the very preciousness of life. Help me to find purpose in this suffering. Thank you for taking flesh and knowing my humanity rather than being a God far-off. Thank you for bearing my sins in your own body and giving me life, not just here on earth, but life eternal and the promise of the resurrection. Thank you for enduring the cross, not being afraid of death, but using death to break death. You've defeated death forevermore by bursting forth from the grave.

> *"O Death, where is your sting? O Hades, where is your victory? The sting of death is sin, and the strength of sin is the law. But thanks be to God, who gives us the victory through our Lord Jesus Christ."*
> *1 Corinthians 15:55–57*

My baby Shalom, I do not know if this is the beginning of your story, or the end. But it is surely not the end of your eternal story, my love. Goodnight, my baby Shalom. May the peace of the Lord be within your heart, whether or not you are within my womb. Amen.

I wake up on Sunday morning. I prepare to handle the many questions that will be asked of me at church, eager to be strengthened by the Lord's body and blood for the tasks ahead, assured of His eternal, undying love that died for me. But, this is so difficult. I want to hide; I don't want to answer people's (well-meaning) questions. I don't even *have* any answers. Perhaps, this is my time to be a receiver of comfort, and let others be blessed by blessing me with their prayers and words of empathy.

> *"Blessed be the God and Father of our Lord Jesus Christ, the Father of mercies and God of all comfort, who comforts us in all our tribulation, that we may be able to comfort those who are in any trouble, with the comfort with which we ourselves are comforted by God." 2 Corinthians 1:3–4*

What to pray for? On the one hand, I want this nightmare to be over, but the easiest way for the end means wishing for the miscarriage to be complete. I certainly don't want that. But I also don't want more unknowns: surgery, sudden death due to a burst fallopian tube, the decision of how to move the baby to where it ought to be in my body. I feel like I'm drowning in the unknowns.

> *"From sudden and evil death, good Lord, deliver us."*

The Scriptures, the liturgy which I know by heart, the hymns are all balm to my soul this morning. They speak truth, regardless of the lies Satan speaks to my heart, or the well-meaning, but inappropriate and misdirected comments people make. The beginning of my tears coincided with the end of the service, and the words of this hymn:

> *Grant us Thy peace, Lord, through the coming night;*
> *Turn Thou for us its darkness into light.*
> *From harm and danger keep Thy children free;*
> *For dark and light are both alike to Thee.*
> *Grant us Thy peace throughout our earthly life,*
> *Our Balm in sorrow and our Stay in strife.*
> *Then, when Thy voice shall bid our conflict cease,*
> *Call us, O Lord, to Thine eternal peace. (ELH 597:3, 4)*

All Sunday, we wait. There's nothing to be done. I have no control over this situation.

> *"I wait for the Lord, my soul waits,*
> *And in His word I do hope." Psalm 130:5*

I wake up on Monday morning and prepare for a doctor's appointment early in the morning. I get my blood drawn again to compare hCG levels. I'm sent to another facility to receive a faster result, but there's some confusion about the order. Phone calls and faxes are flying between offices. The results are in, but I can't have them. They can only be shared with my doctor, but we can't get a hold of my doctor.

I call our cost-sharing ministry and open a need regarding the ER visit. The worker prays with me, acknowledging that no one but God can understand my pain, and He can understand it even better than I myself. This is truth.

And now it's 5 p.m. and offices are closed. And I never received word about whether or not my baby is dead.

I need to leave my phone behind. I walk. Maybe I shouldn't be walking so vigorously? Maybe I should be on bed-rest? But no doctor ordered such a thing. No doctor ordered anything. Nothing. I know nothing.

I walk. Should I walk to my neighbor's and cry on her shoulder? A precious Bible-study friend who has years resulting in wonderful Biblical wisdom and gray hair as her crown of glory? Should I walk to church and pray in the pew, pouring my heart out to God? Church is a block closer, and I end up there, hoping that no one will "bump" into me on my way in and just let me be alone with God. I peek into the empty sanctuary. Sanctuary is just what I need. I putz with the lights, hoping to pray at the altar. But there's a scuffling. And I see a foot peeping out from behind a pillar. I take a step closer. And there is my neighbor, already praying for me. We hug and dissolve in tears. She showed me what she was praying:

> "Out of the depths I cry to you, Lord;
> Lord, hear my voice.
> Let your ears be attentive to my cry for mercy.
> If you, Lord, kept a record of sins,
> Lord, who could stand?
> But with You there is forgiveness,
> so that we can, with reverence, serve you.
> I wait for the Lord, my whole being waits,
> and in His word I put my hope.
> I wait for the Lord
> more than watchmen wait for the morning,
> yes, more than watchmen wait for the morning.

> *Israel, put your hope in the Lord,*
> *for with the Lord is unfailing love*
> *and with him is full redemption.*
> *He Himself will redeem Israel from all their sins."*
> *Psalm 130*

She left me so I could pray. As I sit in the front pew, I sob without words, letting the Holy Spirit interpret my groaning. I want my baby. I want to be healthy. I want to glorify my Father. I want to be obedient. I want my own way.

What are the plans You have for me, and for Shalom, O Lord? How can You give us a hope and future if You take one or both of us?

And the Lord gives me comfort: There is a whole lot more future than just life here on earth. Though I expected to wait nine months to meet my baby, I may have to wait forty or fifty years, but I will, indeed, meet my baby. Heaven is our home. Our hope and our future, eternal togetherness with our Creator, is ultimately there, and is God's ultimate plan for our lives.

God is all-powerful. He can save Shalom's life through doctors and medicine, but He may choose otherwise. But since He is all-powerful, He can do something no doctor or medicine can do: He can redeem us from sin, give His life for ours, raise dead bodies back to life, and gift us an eternal family reunion beyond imagination.

God, You can redeem any person, and You can redeem any situation. There is good in this, though I cannot see it. I give you thanks, O God, for Shalom's life, for life eternal for all of us—now or later. Give glory to yourself, O God, in this situation. Use Shalom's life to bring others to faith.

My crying ceases. I feel God's *shalom*: peace. My family needs me. I walk home.

> *"I know whom I have believed and am persuaded that He is able to keep what I have committed to Him until that Day." 2 Timothy 1:12*

While I was gone, my clever husband figured out how to set up and log on to the hospital's patient portal to "hack" into my own lab results. The hCG was significantly lower, indicating miscarriage; Shalom is in Jesus' arms.

We gather the children around on the couch like every other night, but different. I am reminded that Shalom heard my husband read the Bible every day, heard our hymns and prayers. God's Word does not return to Him void. I tell the children the good news that Mommy does not need to have surgery, and though we will have to wait to meet baby Shalom, we will still meet him or her someday in Heaven. My son interrupts and reminds me that actually Jesus could return any day, so we might not have to wait long at all! My husband shares the name we gave the baby: Shalom, which means peace.

The children are confused. They thought it was Hebrew for "Hello" and "Good-bye." Daddy reassures them that, yes, it is also a Middle Eastern greeting, and the children are thrilled: They can soon say "hello" to Shalom in Heaven, though we have to say "good-bye" for now.

I am touched. That was not the meaning I had intended when I suggested the name to my husband; God has given us a gift and reminder in Shalom's name itself. The children excitedly babble that the baby is at Heaven's party with Jesus. My oldest asks if she can give Shalom a middle name: Hope.

> *"Let us hold unswervingly to the hope we profess,*
> *for he who promised is faithful." Hebrews 10:23*

We agree.

> *"The Lord gives, and the Lord takes away,*
> *blessed be the name of the Lord." Job 1:21*

Lord, have mercy. Christ, come quickly. Amen.

Reprinted, with permission, from
www.hausvater.org/articles/390

Scripture Index

As noted in the introduction, the devotions in this book have been arranged in approximate chronological order, whereas English Bibles group the books somewhat topically (history, wisdom literature, prophecy, etc.). The following index will assist readers in locating devotions that reflect upon particular Bible passages of interest.

Hymn Index

Hymn numbers are listed sequentially, based on the *Evangelical Lutheran Hymnary*, followed by page references to the corresponding devotions. For conversions with other hymnals, see Appendix 2.

This index may serve a variety of purposes. For example, Bible study leaders may wish to first choose a familiar hymn and then use this index in order to find a suitable devotion to share with their ladies' group.

About the Author

Marie K. MacPherson is wife to Ryan, homeschooling hausmutter to their six living children, and redeemed child of God. She is editor of *Mothering Many: Sanity-Saving Strategies from Moms of Four or More* (2016). She has a bachelor's degree in Elementary Education from Bethany Lutheran College, with Lutheran school certification and a specialty in communication arts and literature. She used to actively participate in theater, debate team, choir, and international travel, but realizes now that those were merely a foretaste of the joys of her current vocation: managing children's dramatics, arbitrating kids' arguments, singing hymns and lullabies, and sharing unbelievable mission stories. She has been an advocate for mothers, serving as a La Leche League Leader for over six years and a volunteer at a local pro-life pregnancy clinic. When she's not caring for her own children, or the mothers of other children, Marie reads extensively, researching natural health, healing diets, alternative medicine, dementia, homeschooling, theology, evangelism, marriage, and parenting. Follow her blog at:

www.intoyourhandsllc.com/blog

Ordering Information

Meditations on the Vocation of Motherhood is available for individual purchase at Amazon.com and other reputable booksellers. To inquire about bulk orders for your women's group, contact the publisher at:

www.intoyourhandsllc.com/contact

Also by Marie K. MacPherson

Mothering Many:
Sanity-Saving Strategies
from Moms of Four or More

25 moms of 160+ children navigate 56 challenges that mothers frequently face: menu-planning, laundry, time-management, self-care, homeschooling, intimacy, home-devotions, and much more!

Conceived by one perplexed mom and gestated over eight years, Mothering Many has finally been birthed through a labor of love by dozens of fellow Christian women. Literally written between nursing babies and wiping bottoms, this book offers hundreds of strategies, insights, and ideas for strengthening your home for the Lord. So, if you're too busy from the rigors of motherhood to brainstorm for improvement, crack open this book and let these moms troubleshoot for you!

Bonus sections of this book include: a comparison between the editor's own perspective as a mother of three in 2010 and a mother of five in 2016; a quiz for discovering your own mothering personality; plus insights from seven "mature moms" whose children are now grown and raising children of their own. Discussion questions are provided for use in moms' groups.

To Order:

www.intoyourhandsllc.com/publishing/books

Mothering Many Facebook Group

Did you like what you just finished reading? Eager for more tips and encouragement? Have questions of your own? We'd love to "meet" you! Join the continuing conversation at:

www.facebook.com/groups/motheringmany

Also Published by Into Your Hands LLC

Debating Evolution before Darwinism: An Exploration of Science and Religion in America, 1844–1859, by Ryan C. MacPherson, Ph.D.

Fifteen years before Darwin's *Origin of Species* shook the world, a debate over evolution already raged in America's classrooms, churches, and scientific institutions. Vestiges of Creation, published anonymously by the Scottish journalist Robert Chambers in 1844, boldly marshaled recent scientific discoveries into a sweeping hypothesis of naturalistic development. Crafting a narrative energetic enough for lay readers, but supported with footnotes thorough enough for scholars, Dr. MacPherson reveals unexpected interactions between religion and science during this crucial era.

"Church Control or Birth Control": Margaret Sanger's Propaganda Campaign against the Catholic Church, by Nicholas Kaminsky, M.A.

The name Margaret Sanger is nearly synonymous with birth control in the United States. A controversial character even now, she founded the predecessor to today's Planned Parenthood and dedicated her life to working tirelessly for the legalization and promotion of birth control and abortion. While scholars have directed some attention toward Sanger's provocative statements on race and ethnicity, few have documented her vehement anti-Catholicism or shown the way she cleverly used anti-Catholic propaganda to promote her birth control crusade. Kaminsky has now done so. In this book, he demonstrates the way in which Sanger exploited powerful anti-Catholic sentiment in the United States to portray her fight for birth control as a struggle for American Freedom against a moral domination by the Catholic Church.

Rediscovering the American Republic, Volume 1: 1492-1877 and *Volume 2: 1877–Present*, by Ryan C. MacPherson, Ph.D.

Each volume contains over 700 pages of time-tested teaching tools, collectively spanning ten major epochs of American history: Pre-Columbian to British North America, 1492–1763; The Creation of the American Republic, 1763–1789; The Power of Political Parties, 1789–1836; Liberty, Slavery, and American Destiny, 1836–1860; The Civil War and Reconstruction, 1860–1877; America in the Gilded Age, 1877–1901; Progressive Reform and Human Nature, 1901–1929; The Emergence of the American Superpower, 1929–1953; The Cold War and Civil Rights, 1953–1981; The Triumph and the Vulnerability of the World's Only Superpower, 1981–Present.

Meet Pastor Goodenough: A Humorous Look at Life in the Parish, by Lyle L. Luchterhand.

Little does young Pastor Willie B. Goodenough expect the challenges awaiting him at his first call: All Sports Lutheran Church in Cadaver, Wisconsin. There he meets Betty May, the gossip; Erv Klipstein, the treasurer who is determined not to spend people's offerings on the Lord's work; and I. C. Coldshoulder, the greeter who makes sure church visitors never return. Countless other curmudgeons take turns whisking away their unsuspecting pastor on a whirlwind of unforeseeable, unforgettable, and nearly unforgivable antics. Again and again we're reminded that scoundrels never get past God—or the minister's wife. In this humorous parody of a pastor's life, real-life Pastor Lyle Luchterhand leads his readers from one laugh to another, while Willie's faithful wife Missy reminds us that no matter how crazy the ministry gets, no congregation is ever quite so God-forsaken as it may seem.

www.intoyourhandsllc.com/publishing/books

Into Your Hands LLC

To Stay Informed of
Our Research and Publications:

www.facebook.com/groups/intoyourhandsllc

Coming Soon!

Lessons Learned at Home:
Families Tell Their Homeschooling Stories

Christian home educators offer a unique perspective in today's complicated world of opportunities and decisions. The families represented in this book share their experiences and answer significant questions, including:

Why do some families educate their children primarily in the home, others utilize public or parochial schools, and still others try some of each?

How do Progressive, Classical, Christian, and Unschooling models for education differ from each other, and is it possible to integrate these philosophies into a coherent approach?

What distinctive emphases do Lutheran, Catholic, and Reformed home education resources offer families?

How do home educating parents coordinate their family schedules, select curricula, and track their progress?

What have home educators done to pass muster with state requirements, make use of taxpayer-funded services, and prepare their children for the "real world"?

How can home educators constructively address the concerns of grandparents, pastors, neighbors or others who have doubts about children not being in school?

Where should you turn for more information, without wasting your time in the vast sea of online resources?

Whether you currently home educate your children, would like to do so, or are afraid to try, this book provides the insights you need to make an informed judgment—and to explain your choices to those who think differently.

To volunteer to participate in our homeschool family survey, or to order this book, visit:

www.intoyourhandsllc.com/publishing/books/71b